General Studies Series

ACCEPTABLE QUALITY STANDARDS in the Leather and Footwear Industry

UNITED NATIONS INDUSTRIAL DEVELOPMENT ORGANIZATION
Vienna, 1996

ID/SER.O/20

UNIDO PUBLICATION
Sales No. UNIDO.95.4.E
ISBN 92-1-106301-9

ACCEPTABLE QUALITY STANDARDS IN THE LEATHER AND FOOTWEAR INDUSTRY

CONTENTS

ABBREVIATIONS

AFNOR	Association française de normalisation
ALCA	American Leather Chemists Association
AQEIC	Asociación Química Española de la Industria del Cuero
ARSO	African Regional Organization for Standardization
ASTM	American Society for Testing and Materials
BLC	British Leather Confederation. The Leather Technology Centre (previously BLMRA)
BLMRA	British Leather Manufacturers Research Association
BS	British Standards
BSI	British Standards Institute
CASCO	ISO Committee on conformity assessment
CEC	Commission of the European Community
CEN	Comité européen de normalisation
CTC	Centre technique cuir, chaussure, maroquinerie
DIN	Deutsche Industrie Normen
DIS	Draft International Standard
EC	European Community (previously EEC)
EEC	European Economic Community
EFTA	European Free Trade Association
EMPA	Eidgenössische Materialprüfungs- und Forschunganstalt
EU	European Union
EURIS	European Union of Research Institutes for Shoes
FEICA	Fédération européenne des industries des colles et adhésifs/ Association of European Adhesives Manufacturers
GERIC	Groupe européen de recherches dans les industries du cuir
ICT	International Council of Tanners
ICHSALTA	International Council of Hides, Skins and Leather Traders Associations
IEC	International Electrochemical Commission
ISO	International Organization for Standardization
ITC	International Trade Centre
IULTCS	International Union of Leather Technologists and Chemists Societies
JALCA	Journal of the American Leather Chemists Association
JSLTC	Journal of the Society of Leather Technologists and Chemists
ORAN	Organisation Regionale Africaine pour la Normalisation
PFI	Prüf- und Forschungsinstitut für die Schuhherstellung Pirmasens
PPE	European Personal Protective Equipment

SATRA	Shoe and Allied Trades Research Association
SI	Système international d'unités
SLTC	Society of Leather Technologists and Chemists
TC	ISO technical committee
TG	CEN task group
TNO	TNO Centre for Leather and Shoe Research
VESLIC	Verein Schweizerischer Lederindustrie Chemiker
WG	CEN working group
WGR	Westdeutsche Gerberschule Reutlingen

1. The case for quality control

For a long time, the reputation of leather was based on its properties as a natural product, mainly its comfort, strength and durability. Since the beginning of the century, new and various uses of leather, new raw and auxiliary materials, and new machines have appeared, bringing wide-ranging evolution and change in tanning and leather-utilizing technologies and at the same time a significant increase in the consumption of leather articles.

Under the influence of fashion, the aesthetic properties obtained through dyeing and finishing, design and models have acquired more importance. In the competition with various artificial and synthetic substitutive materials, genuine leather and its derived products are compensating their high prices by aesthetic, comfort, fit and feel properties highly appreciated by consumers. The foot and body protection aspects have lost importance in casual footwear and leather garments, but in safety articles protection requires from leather and leather articles maximum reliance and security. New areas, such as the furniture and car industries, have become substantial users of natural leather. All these factors have increased demand for genuine leather and leather products, with increasing requirements for quality and constant demand for improvement and new variations.

Leather users and consumers need a definition of each of the properties and means to control raw materials, processes and the quality of finished products, as well as of leather articles. Quality and quality control play an important role and are the cornerstones on which the good reputation of leather, tanners, leather products manufacturers and traders are built.

As the distinction between countries supplying essentially raw materials and countries producing leathers on an industrial scale becomes less clear, the developing countries, once exporters solely of raw hides and skins, are encountering growing pressure to improve the quality of their semi-processed and finished leathers and their leather products.

This publication is intended to inform developing countries about quality control and about recommendations for acceptable quality levels for leather, footwear and leather products.

The production of semi-processed and finished leathers of acceptable quality depends on more than the regulation of the manufacturing processes involved. The quality of the raw material and water supply, caliber of the technical and managerial staff, possession and judicious application of apparatus for chemical, physical and fastness testing, availability and quality of chemical supplies, capacities to generate power, regularity of technical service from chemical and machinery suppliers, facilities for in-plant maintenance of equipment and the capacity to manufacture simple process equipment, all significantly affect the quality of a product and its consistency.

The further along in the process sequence towards the finished product, the more production must be controlled. From the raw material stage onwards, precise control becomes essential. Inconsistencies in **one** operation leading to inconsistencies in the subsequent ones can be disastrous. Likewise, faults in any one of the dressing processes can destroy the extra value sought in the production of finished leathers.

Unless tanners in developing countries invest in the broad range of equipment required for producing good finished leathers (process control and test apparatus, efficient and precise machinery, regulated power and water supplies, plant maintenance and construction facilities, and the experienced personnel to operate it) they will remain producers of semi-processed leathers. All raw hides and skins can be sold whether on the home or overseas markets. With semi-processed goods, a small proportion of leathers damaged (possibly while on the animal or by poor take-off, curing, beamhouse work, pickling or tanning) will be unsaleable on the export market but can be used for leather products for the home market.

With finished leathers, the quantity of rejects will increase for several reasons. After basic tanning, processes are tailored more strictly to the properties required in the final leather, whether it is for footwear, clothing, furniture or leather goods. Consequently, the correct selection of leathers in the blue or crust is critical. Incorrect selection of type, grain quality or substance will make the whole batch unsuitable for the purpose intended. In addition, a multitude of faults can occur in the dressing and finishing processes that are either expensive or impossible to correct; hence the need to have a competent workforce to operate the machinery, competent staff to supervise and control the wet and machine processes and reliable facilities to support the whole operation.

Tanners, manufacturers and traders who have an eye on repeat orders will have a concern to improve their quality control.

2. The supply and demand position of leather

The leather industry in the developing world should be aware of the unique position of leather in the market. One factor dominates the whole structure of production and selling. Whatever the demand for leather, the supply of hides and skins remains fixed and beyond the control of the leather manufacturer. For no other major international commodity is one side of the supply demand equation so fixed. Hence, there is absolutely no point in applying normal marketing principles to the marketing of leather, that is, stimulating demand simply to achieve increased turnover of goods and profits. With a fixed supply of raw materials, both production and sales must be geared to increasing the value of the turnover without increasing the volume.

This approach is particularly apposite in view of the possible limitation on the expansion of the world's herds and flocks. Greater emphasis on arable agriculture in North America and western Europe is being proposed as a means of producing protein for human consumption. The view is widely held that the nutritional value of grains fed to animals is higher than that of the meat ultimately produced. Such views gain credence in a world increasingly worried about food supplies. Any marginal growth of the world's population of animals for meat consumption is unlikely to keep pace with the growth of demand for shoes, clothing and other consumer products. Thus, hide and skin supplies may decrease slightly in the future. Furthermore, hide protein may be in growing demand from outside the leather industry. Hitherto, such demand has never been significant, but the increasing need for hide protein as a foodstuff for human consumption and discoveries of new medical and industrial applications for collagen have created a potential demand that could affect the raw material market in the future. The industry, even in the developing world, is re-examining its economic position. It could make a positive contribution towards easing the situation by channelling low-grade hides into non-leather uses, which would result in the upgrading of the leather market as a whole.

The demand for hides and skins is unlikely to decrease. The steep rise in oil prices in the 1970s caused prices for alternative synthetic materials to soar. Leather became more competitive and the preference of consumers in the developed world for leather over synthetics was again demonstrated. Increasing demand for hides and skins, especially in the Far East, intensifies competition on the world market for raw materials, which means continuing unstable prices.

Success for the leather industry in the developing countries, which are now striving to utilize locally the raw hides and skins formerly exported, will depend on their ability to produce to consistently high standards of quality.

Despite the demand for leather products, the production of synthetics is making technical progress, with the result that consumers of leather products are becoming more discretionary in their purchases. Even in developing countries this means that the market for low-grade leathers will be restricted. The existence of such a market is essential for the continuance of a leather industry endeavoring to maintain high standards of quality. If the demand for products of good quality were to become stable, quality standards should be imposed to ensure consumer confidence in the more expensive natural material.

3. Importance of and need for performance standards

Specifications of performance for leathers have largely been subject to agreement between the tanner and the product manufacturer. Although many chemical, physical and fastness tests are available, the number of performance specifications is small. The growth in international trade in leather and leather products calls for the establishment of more definite levels of performance so that the reputation for quality will be protected and developing countries entering the trade will make full use of the technology available.

Official methods of analysis and testing, internationally accepted, are imperative for delineating standards and specifications. International official methods are needed to protect tanner and manufacturer, to avoid trade disputes and misinterpretation and to allow them to sell their leather and products on export markets imposing performance standards.

Two international organizations deal with leather testing: the International Organization for Standardization (ISO) and the International Union of Leather Technologists and Chemists Societies (IULTCS).

The Comité européen de normalisation (CEN) covering the countries of the European Union, previously the European Economic Community (EEC), and the countries of the European Free Trade Association (EFTA), has standardized leather testing methods and also mandatory specifications for performance standards.

Many countries have their national standards bureau, their standardized leather and leather products testing methods and sometimes specifications for performance. Africa has a regional organization for standardization, ARSO-ORAN.

ISO is a worldwide federation of national bodies, the world's largest non-governmental system for voluntary industrial and technical collaboration at the international level. ISO work is decentralized, being carried out by technical committees and subcommittees. The Central Secretariat in Geneva assists in coordinating ISO operations, administers voting and approval procedures, and publishes the International Standards. ISO TC/120 is the technical committee for hides and skins and for leather. ISO TC/45 and TC/137 cover leather and non-leather footwear and TC/176, the quality assurance standards (annex 1).

Most of the ISO technical committees are bureaucratic, and TC/120 has not been particularly active. Recently, the ISO Board of Directors recognized IULTCS as the legal organization specialized in the preparation, definition and drafting of standard testing methods for leather. The ISO Secretariat has also agreed to existing IULTCS methods as official ISO methods after translation into ISO format. Only the standards on raw and semi-processed hides and skins remain in the activities of TC/120.

IULTCS, grouping some 40 countries over the world, has three international commissions working on leather testing:
- IUC, International Commission for chemical analysis
- IUP, International Commission for physical testing
- IUF, International Commission for fastness testing

The commissions are working with leather and footwear institutes and with members of the chemical and tanning industries. They select and study methods, compare and evaluate the results of testing in different laboratories, propose draft methods for adoption by the Council of Delegates at the biennial Congresses of IULTCS. An updated list of methods is given in chapter 4 and annex 2. Some selected methods will be redrafted in ISO format in order to be incorporated into the ISO standards and to replace the existing ISO methods.

In order to avoid possible technical obstacles to a greater competitivity in the markets, the Commission of the European Community has created the CEN standardization committee dealing *inter alia* with leather and leather products, for which CEN/TC 289 has been created. It has three working groups:

WG 1		Terminology
WG 2		Sampling and analysis, subdivided in three task groups:
	TG 1	Chemical tests
	TG 2	Physical/mechanical tests
	TG 3	Fastness tests
WG 3		Guidelines for leather performance

The standardized CEN methods and their quality specifications are mandatory and will be quoted in contracts and specifications. The member countries of the European Union will have to replace their national standards by the adopted CEN standards. Commercial transactions and contracts in the European Union will be specified in terms of CEN methods (annex 3).

During the transition period and also in uses other than commercial transactions, the national standards will still be utilized. The most important are DIN (Deutsche Industrie Normen), BS (British Standards), ASTM (American Standards for Testing Materials), AFNOR (Association française de normalisation) and VESLIC (Verein Schweizerischer Lederindustriechemiker). Annex 4 gives a list of the most important standards for leather and leather products.

The international contracts jointly developed by the International Council of Hides, Skins and Leather Traders' Associations (ICHSALTA) and the International Council of Tanners (ICT) have clauses indicating that in the event of a dispute, measurement of area or chemical analysis has to be carried out in accordance with the official methods of analysis of IULTCS (1) (annex 5).

4. Standards for leather testing

4.1 Selection of tests

To ascertain a leather's overall performance or to establish its suitability for particular end-uses, certain tests must be performed, which will differ according to the end-use. Not all tests need to be performed on all types of leather. It is necessary to determine which tests to use for which leathers.

A distinction has to be drawn between tests on the leather to determine, on one hand, the behaviour of the leather's external appearance (all fastness tests like ageing, light, rub and other tests like flex resistance, finish adhesion) and, on the other hand, the strength of the fibre structure (grain crack, tear, stitch tear, tensile). Tests will also be selected according to the techniques used in the manufacture, e.g. solvent resistance, water absorption, steam and heat resistance, migration, fat content. The end-uses can determine the selection of specific tests like perspiration resistance for linings and some garments, flame resistance for industrial and furniture leathers, fogging for car upholstery leathers.

4.2 Sampling

Due to the heterogeneity of leather, care has to be taken in the sampling, in the number of samples drawn from a lot or a consignment to form a gross sample, in the location of test pieces in each item (hide or skin) and in the number of test pieces. The gross sample should be representative of the lot. The location of sampling, important for physical testing and to some extent for chemical analysis, should be representative of the structure configuration of the leather. The number of test pieces influences the accuracy of the test results.

Sampling should be a compromise between accuracy and reproducibility through taking enough pieces in a valuable location in the skin and, at the same time, avoiding spoiling too much leather. In the future, non-destructive methods for testing mechanical properties will probably be applicable to leather, for example methods based on acoustic emission (2).

The number of pieces in the gross sample and the number of test pieces which need to be selected and tested depends on several factors such as accuracy required and skin-to-skin variability. It is therefore not possible to specify in a standard method what number should be taken. There are statistical methods to determine this number. In practice, the minimum number will be three and for bigger deliveries the following formulas can be used:

$$n = 0.2 \ \sqrt{x} \qquad \text{or} \qquad n = 0.5 \ \sqrt{x}$$

where n is the number of samples and x the number of pieces in a batch. The number of items for a gross sample is also given by ISO 2588.

For physical testing, the sampling method is given by standard IUP 2 and for chemical analysis by standard IUC 2 (ISO 4044). Both methods may be used on finished leather or on leather during processing (lime, pickled, wet blue, crust etc.) The sample pieces should be marked in such a way that their position relative to the backbone can be assessed.

IUP 2, sampling for physical testing, will be merged with IUP 1, general remarks, and drafted in ISO format to replace the existing ISO 2418.

4.3 Preparation of samples for testing

4.3.1 *Cutting test pieces*

Test pieces are cut with cutting knives, which can be made from steel straps used for making cutting dies in the footwear industry, except for heavy leathers for which forged dies are needed.

To obtain cleanly cut test pieces, the cutting knives used must be sharp and clean, without splinters. The angle formed by the cutting edge between the internal and the external surfaces of the press knife and the wedge of this angle are specified in IUP 2/ISO 2418 (formerly IUP 1).

The results of some physical tests depend on the direction (relative to the backbone of the skin or the hide) in which samples are cut. For these tests, the direction of cutting should be specified and tests should be performed in the two directions, perpendicular and parallel to the backbone.

Unless otherwise stated, the knives are applied to the grain surface or to the surface of the leather corresponding to the grain.

4.3.2 *Conditioning*

Many physical properties of leather depend on the water vapour present in the fibre structure. To obtain reproducible results in physical testing, the humidity content of the leather must be maintained constant by storage in a conditioned atmosphere.

The climatic conditioning is specified in method IUP 3 (ISO 2419) and is for a temperature of $20 \pm 2°$ C and a relative humidity of $65 \pm 2\%$. Leather samples and test pieces shall be stored during at least 24 hours in the standard climatic conditions. Most of the tests, certainly those taking a long time, should be performed in the standard atmosphere. In some countries it is difficult to obtain the above conditions, so alternative atmospheres are defined in ISO 554, i.e. $27 \pm 2°$ C and $65 \pm 2\%$ RH or $23 \pm 2°$ C and $50 \pm 2\%$. The DIN 53 303 T method for leather specifies $23 \pm 2°C$ and $50 \pm 6\%$.

However, it should be noted that the numerical values of test results will not necessarily be the same if atmospheres other than the standard reference atmosphere of $20°C$ and 65% are used. Any deviation from these conditions must be mentioned in the test reports.

For conditioning of samples and test pieces, the required relative humidity (RH) can be maintained in a closed space (desiccator) either by use of certain salts in water (in which the solid phase is also present in excess) or by the use of a solution, of given concentration, of sulphuric acid in water.

ISO 4677 specifies methods to measure the percentage of relative humidity in climatic and testing rooms.

4.3.3 *Ageing*

For some purposes, the standard climatic conditions may be modified and the test performed at a different temperature and relative humidity, for example flexing endurance testing at low temperature. However, most of the time, the test pieces are stored in different conditions and the test performed in the standard climatic conditions. Several fastness tests (IUF) specify a method for wetting test pieces. There are also methods for accelerated ageing of the structure or of the finish of leather.

Ageing of leather is usually realized after 5 days storage in an atmosphere of $50 \pm 2°C$ and 100% relative humidity and its effect is evaluated by comparing the results before and after treatment. Hydrolysis conditions are given in DIN 53344/82. A draft IUF 142 method is also proposed for artificial ageing without exposure to light.

The action of chemicals - acids, salts, oils, solvents etc. - on leather structure and finish can be evaluated after treatment of test pieces in given conditions and comparative testing before and after treatment.

Conditions prevailing in the leather transforming industries can also be reproduced on test pieces before or during testing.

4.3.4 *Grinding*

For chemical analysis, leather of all kinds must be ground in a cutter mill. The standard method IUC 3/ISO 4044 specifies the characteristics of the mill; knife velocity and diameter of the mesh of the sieve. It gives also the conditions for drying and conditioning of wet or damp samples of leather. For pickled pelts, see paragraph 4.6.5.

4.4 Physical testing of leather

4.4.1 *IUP/ISO methods*

In addition to methods IUP 2 and IUP 3, 13 IUP methods will be drafted in ISO format and will replace existing ISO methods or become new ISO methods:

IUP 4	Measurement of thickness	ISO	2589
IUP 5	Measurement of apparent density	ISO	2420
IUP 6	Measurement of: a) tensile strength (b) % elongation caused by a specified load (c) % elongation at break	ISO	3376
IUP 7	Measurement of absorption of water	ISO	2417
IUP 8	Measurement of tearing load	ISO	3377

IUP 9	Measurement of distension and strength of grain by the ball burst test (lastometer)	ISO	3379
IUP 10	Water resistance for flexible leather (penetrometer)		
IUP 11	Dynamic waterproofness test for boot and shoe sole leather (permeometer)		
IUP 12	Measurement of resistance to grain cracking	ISO	3378
IUP 15	Measurement of water vapour permeability		
IUP 16	Measurement of shrinkage temperature	ISO	3380
IUP 20	Measurement of the flexing endurance of light leathers and their surface finishes		
IUP 32	Area measurement	ISO	11646
IUP 35	Heat resistance for industrial glove leathers	ISO	11645

Measurement of thickness

The hide or the skin does not have the same thickness over all its cross-section. On heavy leathers thickness differences can reach 25% and on light leathers 20% (3). Thickness of leather can be modified by stretching or compressing, by splitting, shaving, buffing or skiving. As many properties depend on the thickness, this will be measured in order to express the test results in relation to the thickness. The measured thickness of a leather depends upon such factors as the pressure and the time for which the pressure is applied. Standard IUP 4/ISO 2589 gives the method for measurement of thickness and specifies the characteristics of the measuring gauge. The results of the thickness measurement are expressed in millimeters to the nearest 0.01 mm.

In routine testing, spring-loaded measuring gauges are frequently used. Their readings, however, are liable to change with time, and it is therefore necessary to calibrate them periodically by comparing their readings with those of a gauge of the standard type.

To evaluate the mechanical properties of leathers in relation to the end-uses, mainly footwear manufacture, the most important tests are the measurement of resistance of grain in the lastometer (IUP 9), tear resistance (IUP 8) and flexing endurance (IUP 22).

Ball burst test

The ball burst test is intended particularly for use with shoe upper leather where it gives an evaluation of the grain resistance to cracking during top lasting of the shoe uppers. The distension at grain crack is expressed in millimeters to the nearest 0.1 mm. The resistance of the grain to cracking depends on the humidity content of the leather; the test is performed on conditioned leather. Low results can give good information for the shoe manufacturer about the need to humidify, damp or wet the leather before lasting. Distension of grain by ball burst can also be performed at higher temperatures to reproduce the conditions of some modern techniques in the footwear industry (heat-setting, hot air treatment to remove wrinkles). Patent leathers are very sensitive to heat treatments, especially in the perforations and in the stitch holes; they can be tested on a lastometer in which the ball is replaced by a half sphere (4). Stitch holes are made in the leather sample before fixing it in the lastometer. A distension of 7.7 mm is given to the leather and the surface of it is heated at 100°C for 3 minutes by a hot air stream. No crack in the patent layer and no tear at the stitch holes is allowed. The lastometer, like the tensometer (see IUP 13) or the plastometer (see IUP 21), gives a progressive distension to the leather. In practice, the distension given to the leather during lasting in shoe manufacture is very fast. The Dutch Leather Institute (TNO) has developed a testing device that better reproduces shoe factory conditions (5).

Resistance to tear

The resistance to tear is very important for all kinds of upper leathers. The official method IUP 7/ISO 3377 measures the tear load on a specimen in which a slot has been cut and which is slipped over the turned-up ends of a pair of holders attached to the jaws of a tensile strength machine. The forces exerted during separation of the holders are recorded and the highest force is taken as the tearing load and expressed in newtons (see annex 5). The initial load and the mean load can also be taken from the recorded diagram. Tearing load can be expressed as the quotient of the load by the thickness of the sample. Another tear resistance test is often used when the available leather sample is very small or when the test has to be performed on manufactured leather articles. It is known as the slit tear test (DIN 53329 or AFNOR G-52004). The test piece is cut lengthwise, an incision is made in the leather, the two ends of the slit are fixed in the jaws of the tensile strength machine and the tearing load is recorded. It is obvious that the load recorded for the slit tear is more or less half of the load recorded during the IUP test. The stitch tear test is also very useful (DIN 53331). In this test a needle or a knife is driven into the leather at 5 mm from the edge of a test piece and the force to tear it out of the leather is recorded and expressed in newtons (annex 6).

Values obtained from the various tear resistance tests give reliable information to the leather products manufacturers on the need for reinforcing during manufacture of leather articles.

Flexing endurance

Flexing endurance of light leathers and their surface finishes (IUP 20) is partly a physical test, but as it is applied mainly for testing the finishes it is also a fastness test. The apparatus used for this test is known as the Bally Flexometer. The test may be performed on conditioned leather samples or on wet samples, in standard climatic conditions or in a cold atmosphere. Some criticism was raised recently because the test is not representative of how leather is flexed during wearing.

Tensile strength

In the measurement of tensile strength (IUP 6/ISO 3376) the medium specimen is normally used for testing light leathers. To prevent the specimen from slipping out of the jaws during the test, it is useful to increase the area of the leather fixed within the jaws from 20 to

30 mm in length and 20 to 25 mm in width and to change the cutting knives accordingly. Constant clamp loads are generated automatically with pneumatic jaws. To avoid breaking near the jaws, a proposal was made to change the shape of the test piece and to give it curved sides.

Behaviour of leather against water

The behaviour of leather against water is evaluated through static methods (IUP 7, measurement of absorption of water by volume or the gravimetric method BS 3144 - SLP 19) or through dynamic methods (IUP 10, water resistance for flexible leathers, and IUP 11, dynamic waterproofness test for boot and shoe sole leather).

The static methods have some interest for sole leathers and the dynamic methods need to be updated. A well-known method for testing upper leather waterproofness is the Maeser method (ASTM D 2099) (6).

Comfort and hygienic properties

For evaluation of comfort and hygienic properties, water vapour absorption (WVA) and water vapour permeability (WVP) are the most important. IUP 15 measures the water vapour permeability and IUP 30 the water vapour absorption and desorption and the related changes of dimensions of leather. For WVA, there is also the DIN 4843 static method and for both WVA and WVP, the SATRA PA test (7) as well the AFNOR kinetic G 52-019 method (8).

Measurement of area

Established in agreement with the International Council of Tanners, IUP 32, measurement of area, is used to check the area of flexible leathers. The machine used is a pin-wheel machine with specified transport rollers speed and distance between pins of two adjacent pin wheels.

4.4.2 *IUP methods that will not be converted to ISO*

Several IUP methods became obsolete or were seldom in use. They can be applied for some specific purposes or research activities and are kept as IUP (see list in annex 2). Two draft methods are under testing, waiting for official approval.

IUP 26, determination of the abrasion resistance of sole leather, will replace the previous method, which uses very expensive equipment. The draft method is similar to the abrasion test on rubber and to the DIN 53516 method; apparatus and auxiliary materials are described in ISO 4649.

IUP 33, fogging test, is intended for car upholstery leathers. Fogging refers to the condensation of vaporized volatile particles from car interior fittings onto car windows, particularly the windscreen (DIN 75 201), and is considered a safety hazard (9) (10). Many car manufacturers have their own method, with differences in temperatures, time and conditions under which the test is run; the results are gravimetric or expressed in reflectance (11).

4.4.3 *Deleted IUP methods*

Three IUP methods were deleted because they were no more in use or because more reliable information can be obtained by other methods:

IUP 22   The assessment of damage by use of the viewing box
IUP 23   The measurement of surface damage by an impact
IUP 28   Measurement of the resistance to bending of heavy leather

4.4.4 *Some other physical methods*

Softness test

An important organoleptic property of leather is its softness, traditionally evaluated subjectively by experienced graders, tanners and leather transformers. A more objective evaluation giving a numerical value to leather softness was developed by the British Leather Confederation (12). It is a non-destructive method utilizing a portable gauge called a softness tester, which measures the extent to which a leather will stretch when a fixed load is applied to it, perpendicular to the plane of the leather. The device works on a similar principle to the lastometer, clamping and applying a load to the leather with the resultant distension giving an indication of leather softness. The load applied is typically on the order of 500 g and does not cause any damage to the leather. The IULTCS Physical Testing Commission is proposing a draft for a method to be standardized (annex 7).

Testing flame resistance

Fire and flame resistance are required of materials used in furniture (13), and in automobile and aircraft seat covers as well as safety and protective garments and equipment. The widespread employment of leather in upholstery and the increased work safety regulations implies the production of leather with good flame resistance.

The vertical flame test (DIN 53438 - BS 2782) is the most widely used; it is easy to perform on a strip of leather suspended vertically in a draught-free atmosphere. A gas flame is placed under one edge of the leather sample for 12-15 seconds and then removed. The time in seconds that the material continues to burn and the time the material continues to burn without flame afterglow are noted together with the char length, the length of the strip that is burnt and the part of the sample that breaks.

Horizontal tests are similar (ALCA E 50 - DIN 75200) but less severe. The flame is positioned on one of the surfaces of the leather for 12 or 15 seconds and the time before a hole appears, the length of the after-flaming and the length of the afterglow are noted.

More severe tests are the cigarette and match test of BS 5852/Part 1, where an ignited cigarette and/or the flame of a match are placed in contact with the leather, and the crib test of BS 5852/Part 2, where the leather is placed in a wooden crib in which alcohol is burnt.

Other tests use oxygen index, e.g. ASTM D 2863 measuring the minimum amount of oxygen concentration required to support candle-like combustion.

4.5   Fastness testing

The letters IUF (International Union Fastness) mark the standard methods of testing and standards for methods of testing prepared by the International Fastness Test Commission.

Directives and test specifications are classified in four groups:

GROUP 1   with the numbers 100-199 comprises general information, principles, assessment scales, preparation of standard substrates.

GROUP 2   with the numbers 200-299 comprises testing the properties of dyestuffs and finishing material without the aid of leather

GROUP 3   with the numbers 300-399 comprises testing the properties of dyestuffs and finishing material upon application to leather.

GROUP 4   with the numbers 400-499 comprises colour fastness testing of leather.

The ISO Secretariat has agreed to existing IUF methods as official ISO methods after translation into ISO format.

Annex 2 gives the list of IUF methods.

The most important fastness tests, applicable to nearly all types of leather, are rub fastness and pigment adhesion, followed by fastness to light.

4.5.1   *The colour fastness to cycles of to-and-fro rubbing (IUF 450 - ISO 11640)*

The colour fastness to cycles of to-and-fro rubbing (IUF 450 - ISO 11640) needs an apparatus known as the FEK-VESLIC tester on which the leather to be tested is rubbed with pieces of standard white or coloured wool felt (14) under a given pressure with a given number of forward and backward motions. In the test, the felt may become more or less coloured through transfer of any kind of coloured matter, e.g. finish, pigment, dyestuff and buffing dust and the colour and surface of the leather may become altered. The change in colour of the felts and of the leather is assessed with the standard grey scales. The test can be performed on dry leather with dry felt, on dry leather with wet felt and on wet leather with dry felt. Leather and felt may be wetted with demineralized water or with an artificial perspiration solution.

The rubbing element may be replaced by cotton fabric or by a rubber finger (VESLIC method C 4505) or a rubber strap (15) or abrasive paper (VESLIC 4510)(16). For all those non-ISO/IUF methods, the device for fixing the rubbing element must be adapted.

With the same rub tester, the fastness of the leather surface to waxes, polishes, cleaning products etc. can be evaluated. Fastness of leather and finishes to solvents can be tested on the leather surface or by migration through the leather from fleshside to grain.

Fastness to buffing of dyed leather is tested with a buffing paper of specified grit on the rub fastness tester; it is a standard method IUF 454.

The same apparatus can also be used for testing the colour fastness of leather to ironing (IUF 458). The behaviour of the colour of leather on exposure to a hot iron, as for instance in crease removal in shoe manufacture or ironing in garment manufacture, is evaluated and the highest permissible temperature is the temperature at which the finish does not smear and the colour of the leather remains substantially unchanged. For this test the apparatus need to be equipped with a special metal finger that can be heated at selected temperatures in a range 80° to 240°C. The test is discontinued where a leather irons successfully at 240°C. If leather for shoe uppers cannot be ironed at 80°C, another heating method for crease removal should be recommended, for instance hot air blowing, for which the Föhn test (17) can be applied.

4.5.2 *Test for adhesion of finish, (IUF 470-ISO/11644)*

The adhesion of the finish to the leather or to a lower layer of the finish is measured with the IUF method 470[*] (ISO 11644). Dependent on the way the leather has been finished, the adhesion of the finish to the leather can be so low that the finish separates from the leather during use. With finishes consisting of several layers, the separation may occur between the layers. This method is valid for all leathers with a smooth surface which have been finished and the surface of which can be made to adhere without penetration of the adhesive. The finished side of one part of a strip of leather is stuck to a carrier (in hard PVC) by means of a solvent-free adhesive. The force required to pull the finish away from the underlaying leather is the adhesion and is expressed in newtons per 10 mm width of strip. The adhesion is determined with a tensile machine (18) equipped with a recorder. In the evaluation of the results of the test, it is important to comment on the appearance of the leather after the test, especially the way in which the finish has separated, e.g. separation of the film from the leather, or separation between individual layers of the finish, or tearing of the leather, presence of fibers or part of the grain on the separated finish film. The type of adhesive is important. The polyurethane adhesive used in the new method is free of solvent at the time of application to the finish and has, thus, a very high viscosity. It also stays viscous for only a few seconds and there is no time for penetration of even very thin finishes, unless there are open cracks present. As there can be a relation between adhesion and flexing endurance, the adhesion test should always be performed if flexing endurance fails.

4.5.3 *Colour fastness of leather to light*

Colour fastness of leather to light is evaluated to daylight (IUF 401) or to artificial light under the Xenon lamp (IUF 402); for both the assessment is made with the grey scales (IUF 131 and 132) and by comparing the fading of the leather with that of standard blue wool cloths. The lightfastness of leather, mainly white and light-coloured, depends more on the chemicals used in tanning and finishing, e.g. chrome, vegetable colour, syntans, fat liquors etc. and their interaction, than on dyes and pigments.

---

[*]   A similar test had been proposed in 1975 but never accepted as an official method. In that previous method, the recommended adhesive (Araldite) frequently penetrates the finish films and thus increases the measured values unrealistically; finishes with insufficient adhesion to the adhesive also occur quite frequently. Further, it is usually not possible to measure wet adhesion, as there is insufficient adhesion to the metal carrier when water is present and the speed of separation on the tensile machine is 50 mm/min, whilst all other leather tests with tensile machines specify the speed of 100mm/min. Therefore a polyurethane adhesive, a PVC carrier and the standard speed of separation are recommended in the new method.

Fading can also occur in the dark and during storage of the leather or leather articles and is influenced by the temperature (19). It is useful to combine the lightfastness test with an ageing at higher temperature (DIN 53341). A draft IUF 142, artificial ageing, is also proposed.

4.5.4 *Fastness of leather to water*

IUF 420 is intended for assessing the effect on leather caused by spotting with water. The method gives also a procedure for reproducing ring marks or patches under the finish layer of patent leathers.

IUF 421 - ISO 11642 evaluates the resistance of the colour of leather to the prolonged action of water. A wetted piece of specified undyed textile is placed in contact with a wetted specimen of leather. The composite sample is left under pressure for a specified time in a Hydrotest or Perspirometer apparatus. After drying, change in colour of the leather and staining of the textile are observed.

IUF 423 assesses the colour fastness to mild washing. It was first declared official in 1973, in 1993 a revision was approved to make the method as similar as possible to IUF 435, machine washing. A specimen of the leather and accompanying textile together with Teflon rods are agitated in a washing float, rinsed, squeezed and dried. The change in colour of leather and accompanying textile are assessed and, if applicable, any changes in the finish are noted.

IUF 435 is intended for determining the resistance of leather in a washing machine. It was developed mainly to test leathers used as labels on textile garments and sport footwear. The method is suitable to assess the colour changes of the leather and staining of the accompanying textile and also for conditioning the leather for assessing the change of any other physical or chemical property during machine washing.

4.5.5 *Colour fastness to perspiration (IUF 426 - ISO 11641)*

In many leather articles, the leather comes in direct contact with the human skin. Not only gloving, clothing or lining leathers but also upper leather for unlined shoes and various belt, strap or orthopedic leathers. Human perspiration can also migrate through garment and be absorbed by the leather, causing staining or changes of the leather appearance.

Since there are great individual variations in perspiration, it is not possible to design a method with universal validity, but the alkaline artificial perspiration specified in this method does give results corresponding with those with natural perspiration in most cases. In general, human perspiration is weakly acid when freshly produced. Micro-organisms then cause it to change to weakly alkaline. Alkaline perspiration has a considerably greater effect on the colour of leather than has acid perspiration. Since the more demanding fastness test gives the limiting result, use of an acid perspiration liquor is omitted.

4.5.6 *Fastness to dry cleaning*

IUF 434 - ISO 11643, dry cleaning of small samples, is intended for determining the resistance of the colour and the finish of unused and not yet dry-cleaned leather to dry cleaning solutions. It does not cover composites or complete leather garments. It should not be used to give the dry cleaner any guidelines for the process to be employed for cleaning. A specimen of the leather, together with an accompanying textile and Teflon rods, is agitated in a solvent* which may contain triolein and a detergent, then squeezed and dried at ambient temperature. The change in colour of the specimen and of the accompanying textile are assessed and changes in the finish are noted. As the samples are too small, changes of leather properties, such as handle or area stability, are not considered.

4.5.7 *Artificial ageing*

Most leathers are tested soon after production and it is assumed that the results obtained will be maintained indefinitely both in use and storage. Unfortunately this is not always true. The effects of ageing depend both on the nature of the leather and on the conditions of storage or use. The conditions described in this standard simulate some of those which are known to affect certain leathers in practice. They are not comprehensive and other conditions may also be used, but these conditions offer a good starting point for assessing the possible effects of ageing.

At a later time, when more research has been conducted, it may be advantageous to expand the section on chemical ageing to include the action of chemicals such as ozone, nitrous oxides and sulphur dioxide.

In the draft method IUF 142, the ageing is assessed by performing some physical or fastness test before and after an ageing treatment and reconditioning of the leather. The leather is exposed to elevated temperatures and atmospheres that contain moisture. By chemical ageing, according to this draft method, is to be understood the action of an atmosphere that is almost saturated with water vapour and contains small amounts of ammonia, at elevated temperatures.

This method is applicable to leathers, especially furniture leathers, that are exposed to perspiration or other emissions that cause hydrolysis.

4.5.8 *Migration test and resistance to perspiration*

In the manufacture of leather articles, leather comes in close contact with a variety of other materials. Some components migrate from one to the other material. The best known examples are the migration of plasticizers from soling materials, from adhesives or from nitrocellulose finishes, migration of amines from polyurethanes and migration of dyes from leather to soling materials or to the other accompanying leathers.

The IUF 442 method evaluates the transfer of colour from leather to plasticized polyvinylchloride. The applied procedure can be adapted to other materials.

Similar to migration is the bleeding of dyes or the migration of salt through water from one material to the other, for instance migration of dyes from upper leather to lining, of salt from insole to upper, of vegetable tannin from soles to upper. A very simple and easy not standardized testing method, known as the Streifentest (20) (strip test) gives interesting

---

* To take into account environmental legislation concerning the solvents which are to be used, this method will be revised.

information about these phenomenon. A leather test piece in contact with a filter paper on the surface to be tested (annex 8) is inserted between two glass plates, one small end of the composite sample is dipped in demineralized water, the migration of the water through the leather transfers the soluble matters into the filter paper which after drying will show the results of the migration. The same method can be used to study the effect of migration of artificial perspiration (21).

The structure and colour of leather are sensitive to human perspiration, which attacks the structure and combination tannin with hide substance and changes the colour of dyed leathers. Since there are great individual variations in the pH and composition of human perspiration (22-23), it is difficult to prepare a standard artificial perspiration. In addition, when human perspiration is absorbed by the leather, various reactions can occur depending on factors such as materials present in the leather, intensity and duration of wetting, conditions of drying etc. To test the resistance of the structure of leather to perspiration, the Grassmann and Stadler method (24) and the Herfeld and Härtewig method (25) are often in use. To test the colour fastness of leather, method IUF 426 using an alkaline artificial perspiration gives, in most of the cases, results corresponding to those with natural perspiration.

4.6 Chemical analysis

4.6.1 *Leather chemical analysis*

With the development of mechanical, physical and fastness testing, chemical analysis lost its importance in quality control and evaluation of leather. Nevertheless it remains useful to explain some failures such as brittleness of grain or structure due to low humidity or fat content, exudation and spew due to high salt content or type of fat, sole adhesion difficulties due to fat content, etc.. It can also determine type and amount of chemicals present in the leather or verify the agreement with specifications, requirements or regulations (pH range, formalin, preservative content).

Most of the IUC methods (annex 2) were revised and adapted to the ISO format and will become ISO methods.

The analytical results of a full analysis of leather consist of an analytically determined fraction and a calculated fraction (IUC 1).

Leather samples (location and identification IUC 2 - ISO 2418) for analysis need to be ground (IUC 3 - ISO 4044) in order to have a more homogeneous sample and a better contact between leather and the reagents.

The main chemical determinations are volatile matter, substances soluble in dichloromethane, water solubles and total ash.

Volatile matter in leather (IUC 5)

Volatile matter in leather (IUC 5) is determined by drying the leather at a temperature of $100 \pm 2°C$ to constant weight. This method is usually the first determination in a leather analysis because the results of other analytical determinations are expressed on dry leather.

As leather contains volatile matter other than water, this method gives only an evaluation of the moisture content. Moisture in leather acts as a lubricant and has an influence on the mechanical properties of the leather structure. Moisture content has to be checked during leather production and also during the manufacture of leather articles. There are not-standardized simpler and faster methods, namely infra-red or microwave drying combined with a weighing balance and, as quick control test, the non-destructive conductivity method based on the resistance posed by moisture to an electric current passing between two electrodes applied on the surface of leather (or in it with needle electrodes). Unfortunately the salt content of the leather increases the conductivity and leads to higher moisture content measurement.

Fats and other substances soluble in dichloromethane (IUC 4 - ISO 4048)

In addition to natural fats present in the raw hide or skin, leather contains fats introduced during the tanning process. The type, quantity, repartition and fixation of fat can cause adhesion difficulties in footwear manufacture, troubles in dry-cleaning of leather garment or fatty spew on leather articles. The determination of fat (IUP 4 - ISO 4048) is based on extraction with an organic solvent. Fat bound to the leather is not extracted, but the solvent can dissolve non-fatty substances. The extract can be used for further analysis such as determination of acid and saponification value. The dichloromethane solvent which has been used once can be used again after distillation; due to its toxicity care should be taken to avoid associated hazards. For routine determinations, petroleum ether, boiling point 50-80°C, is safer. Many fat liquors adhere or fix firmly to the fibers; they can be partly extracted with other solvents or solvent mixtures, e.g. n-hexane in the AFNOR NF G 52-204 or ASTM D 3495 methods. To determine combined fat - in chamois leather for instance - solvent-extracted leather is hydrolysed in alcoholic potassium hydroxide and the fat is extracted from the residue (26).

Water-soluble substances in leather (IUC 6)

Water-soluble substances in leather (IUC 6) are defined as the quantities of all those substances, which under certain conditions are dissolved out of the leather by water. These are principally unfixed organic colour, non-colour and mineral salts. The water-soluble inorganic substances (mineral) are defined as the sulphated ash of water-soluble substances; water-soluble organic substances are defined as the difference between total water solubles and water-soluble inorganic substances. The procedure to determine the inorganic water soluble substances includes ashing. The amounts of mineral substances found by ashing can differ from the actual content owing to decomposition, reduction or the escape of certain salts. By treating the ash with sulphuric acid, most of the salts and oxides are converted into sulphates (SAWS, sulphated ashes of water solubles), which give a better evaluation of the actual salt content. Because of their volatility, ammonium salts have to be determined separately. During wear, leather articles are often in contact with water; soluble matter is then extracted and will afterwards dry on the leather surface, causing the well-known white exudations if mineral salts are present, for stains if unfixed tannin and non-colour causing overtanning, hardening and grain cracks are present. In footwear, due to the movement during walking, the soluble substances migrate to the folds of the shoe where their high concentration accelerates the destruction process. Textiles from lining contain also soluble matter from starch and fillers that can give some discolorations mainly on aniline leathers. Perspiration also migrates through the leather and mixes with the other soluble substances causing pH changes, discoloration, mildew and mould.

Acidity or alkalinity of the aqueous leather extract (IUC 11 - ISO 4045)

The acidity or alkalinity of the aqueous leather extract IUC 11 - ISO 4045 is determined by the hydrogen or hydroxyl ions activity with the conventional pH scale. The strength of acids or bases is given by the **difference figure** which is the difference between the pH value of a solution and its tenfold dilution. If the difference figure amounts to 0.7 to 1.0 a solution contains a free strong acid or a free strong base. The majority of tanned leathers is in the acidic range. Presence of acid in leather is not so harmful for the leather itself but it is often dangerous for the textile materials used in combination with leather in the manufacture of leather articles.

Determination of total ash (IUC 7 - ISO 4047)

The residue left from burning leather at a given temperature is called total ash. In addition to the salts present in the leather (solubles and insolubles), the ash contains mineral colours, such as chrome, aluminium, and zirconium. The residues obtained after extracting the leather with water, ashing and sulphating are called water insoluble ash. With the introduction of cleaner technologies and the reduction of water consumption in tanneries, the salt content in leather tends to be high because of replacing of rinsing by washing and working in short floats. Hence the importance of salts determination in the water extract or in the ashes of leather.

Chrome tanning compounds

Chrome tanning compounds (IUC 8) in leather or in tanning baths and materials are determined and calculated as chromic oxide (Cr_2O_3) by the perchloric acid method or the fusion method. There are also other methods using special equipment, such as photometry, atomic absorption spectroscopy, X-ray determination (27). A draft photometric method (IUC 18) for chromium (VI) using 1.5-diphenylcarbazide is proposed.

Other mineral tanning compounds

Other mineral tanning compounds are determined by IUC 13 for zirconium and IUC 16 -ISO 5400 for aluminium. There is also a complexometric titrimetric method for combined determination of zirconium and aluminium (28).

4.6.2 *Vegetable tanning materials and syntans*

There are no agreed international methods (29). Two sets of national methods are official, the ALCA A1, A10 to A13 and A20 and the SLTC 2/1 to 2/3 and 2/3(a) to (k), both shake methods. The filter bell method is still in use in some European countries. All those methods are empirical and the results depend on precise conditions of test.

Various methods (30) (31) are proposed for the evaluation of syntans and retanning baths, e.g. an ultra-filtration and UV spectroscopic quantitative technique (32), a colorimetric method for estimation of acrylic syntans strength (33) and several fluorescence (34) and chromatographic identifications (35).

4.6.3 *Preservatives*

For the protection of the environment, various regulations prohibit or limit the presence of pesticides and preservatives in leather (36). A standard method of determining low levels of pentachlorophenol (PCP) is in preparation for submission to ISO for its approval (37) (38). A ground sample of leather is extracted with a polar solvent and after clean-up of the extract, PCP (and other phenols present) are converted to the acetyl derivative. The acetylated phenols are separated by gas chromatographily detected and quantified. An analytical method for determination of PCP in leather, prepared by the German Footwear Institute (PFI) is standardized by the German Standard Institute DIN No. 53 313 E 10/93 (39). The Spanish Footwear Institute (INESCOP) has also proposed a method based on successive extraction and measurement of PCP by absorbance (40).

The alternative chemical substitutes for PCP are still under evaluation for their effects on health and the environment (41). The diversity of chemicals currently in use for curing either raw or semi-processed hides renders the identification and dosage very difficult (42).

4.6.4 *Other chemicals and auxiliary products*

Determination of the proteolytic activity of enzymes

The IUC 20 draft method is the Lohlein-Volhard method and compares the activity of enzymes at pH 8.2 on a casein substrate. It is quantitative for enzymes of the same type and should not be used for the comparison of different types (pancreatic or bacterial) or active in other pH ranges (soaking or liming).

Hide powder and collagen-rich substitutes were proposed as a substrate for assay of the proteolytic activity of enzymes. A dye is coupled or imbedded in the substrate, making a quick colorimetric evaluation possible (43).

Properties of dyes and finishing materials

The IUF group 2 methods with numbers in the 200s are for testing the properties of dyes and finishing materials (solubility, stability to acid, to alkali, to hardness, to electrolytes).

There are also spectroscopic (44) (45) colorimetric DIN 55 978 (43) methods as well as simple inexpensive test methods like the filter paper dipout (DIN 53 242 Teil 1 + Teil 4) (46) for dyes, the cardboard spray for pigments (47) (48) and various methods proposed by the chemical industry.

The working group Leather Auxiliary Products of the German Federation of Textile, Leather, Tannins, and Washing Auxilliaries (TEGEWA) has a set of specifications for finished binders, pigment, auxiliaries and lacquers based on DIN analytical determinations and testing (49).

Chemicals used in the tannery processes can be hazardous to health. A relatively simple analytical test using thin layer chromatography (50) was proposed for the detection of benzidine in leather dyes and dye mixtures, in addition to procedures (51).

4.6.5 *Analysis of pickled pelt*

Because of the presence of salt and to keep the salt/acid equilibrium, pickled pelts have to be analyzed without oven drying. The analysis method widely in use is the SLTC method of the British Society of Leather Technicians and Chemists (52). It includes determination of the moisture content by distillation in presence of a water-immiscible solvent (n-heptane GPR) in the Dean Stark apparatus; determination of the sodium chloride content by silver nitrate titration; determination of pH of aqueous extract and titrable acidity; determination of substances soluble in dichloromethane; IUC 4 with the fatty extract; determination of free fatty acid, and determination of collagen content expressed as the dry residue after removal of acid, salt and grease. The results are calculated either as a percentage of pelt weight or as a percentage of collagen weight. Shrinkage temperature is determined according to IUP 16.

5.   Standards for footwear testing

5.1   International standards

5.1.1   *ISO standards*

The existing ISO standards for footwear cover a shoe size system known as MONDOPOINT. ISO standards are also related to rubber and plastic footwear and rubber soling materials (annex 1).

The ISO standards for testing conditions and quantities and units are obviously applicable to testing of footwear and footwear materials.

5.1.2   *IULTCS/ISO standards*

The IULTCS/ISO standards (annex 2) are applicable to all types of leather used in the manufacture of footwear and leather articles.

5.1.3   *CEN standards*

For the time being, CEN standards relate to safety footwear and equipment (annex 3). They were prepared by the CEN TC 161 Committee according to the Personal Protective Equipment (PPE) Directive of the EEC .

Testing standards for leather with specification for performances are in preparation by the CEN/TC 289 Committee.

Testing standards for footwear were prepared by the CEN Committee 978 for footwear and its components and are under examination by Working Group 71, on footwear.

5.1.4   *FEICA standards*

The Association of European Adhesives Manufactures (FEICA), in cooperation with the European Footwear Institutes (EURIS), has prepared testing methods for adhesives (annex 3).

5.1.5   *EURIS standards*

The EURIS group of the European Footwear Institutes standardized a set of testing methods on various materials used in footwear manufacture (annex 3).

5.2   National standards

Many countries have their national standards for testing footwear and footwear materials, mainly adhesives and soling materials. Annex 4 gives some of them. The most comprehensive testing methods are the French AFNOR, the British BS and the German DIN standards.

5.3   Testing soling materials

The most important tests on soling materials made of compact or cellular elastomers (natural or synthetic rubbers, PVC, PVA, EVA, PU etc.) are the following:

- Elasticity, elongation and compression. Tensile strength, tear and split tear before and after ageing (AFNOR NF-G-62006 - BS 5350 2.6 - DIN 53504, 53506 - see also ISO 37). For these tests, size and shape, cutting and preparation of test pieces are different from that of leather, but testing conditions are usually the same (BS 5350 2.7).

- Flexing endurance on soles and on combination sole/insole. The most used testing method is the De Mattia (DIN 52 522), where the flexing amplitude can be adapted to the thickness of the materials and samples. The flexing is performed at a speed of 125-150 flexes per minute. To evaluate damage during wear, the growth of a 2 mm cut is observed during flexing. Another well known method is the Satra Ross flexing also with cut growth (BS 5350 2.1. -ISO 6907:1984).

- Abrasion. The German DIN 53 516 is widely in use for soling materials. Round samples of the material to test are abraded under constant pressure (1 kg for compact materials and 0.5 kg for microcellular materials) on a rotating roller covered with a standardized abrasive paper for a distance of 40 metres. The loss of weight of the sample is recorded and expressed in cubic millimetres after determination of the specific weight of the material (weight per cubic cm). During testing, the abrasive strength of the abrasive paper is checked with a standardized rubber material.

- Shore Hardness A or D (DIN 53 505) or hardness, IRHD (ISO 48).

- Suitability of soling materials for adhesives and adhesion. One testing method is the EEC-A1 method for adhesive.

- Fat, oil and plasticizer content and exudation of greasy components. Such materials can migrate during storage or ageing, create adhesion difficulties and require special preparation of the soles before adhesive application. They also can attack the adhesive films before reactivation or destroy the adhesive bond during storage or wear of the shoes.

- Rubber and fillers content. Through chemical analysis, extraction and incineration, the non-rubber or non-elastomeric byproducts that could have negative effects on the quality and behaviour of the soling materials can be determined.

5.4   Testing adhesives

Adhesion problems are still the main troublemakers in footwear manufacture and wear. The British Footwear Institute (SATRA) estimates that poor footwear adhesion leads to the return of over two million pairs of shoes annually in the United Kingdom (53).

Poor adhesion can come from the materials, from the adhesives and/or from the assembly process. All footwear materials have to be prepared by roughing, scouring, degreasing, cleaning or halogenation before application of the adhesives; some materials have a low structural strength and can split in their cross-section. Adhesive type and preparation have to be selected. Application, drying and reactivation of adhesive, bonding and pressing have to be carefully controlled. Evaluation of the chemical, physical and bonding properties helps in predicting the performance and reliability of an adhesive bond. The vital factors in the evaluation of footwear and leather goods adhesives are viscosity, solids content, and most of all, bond strength.

The European Footwear Institutes (EURIS) and the European Federation of Adhesive Manufacturers proposed testing methods (annex 5) to determine the bonding properties of adhesives (EEC A1), the ability of the materials to be bonded (EEC A2) and the strength of the bonds (EEC A3 to 5). Adhesives are tested on standardized materials and/or on materials used in production. Peel strength and shear strength, eventually combined with heat resistance (creep test), are performed in specified conditions for preparing the surface prior to application of adhesive, for preparation of adhesive (mixing, addition of activators or catalysts, melting temperature etc.), for application and drying of the adhesive (thickness of the film, number of coats to be applied, open time, drying conditions etc.), for curing and bonding conditions (reactivation, temperature, pressure, time etc.), for ageing before testing the bond. The strength of the adhesive bond is measured on a tensile machine equipped with a recorder. Peel and shear strength are expressed in newtons/cm width and from the resulting graphs, initial, maximum, minimum and mean value can be calculated. In addition, the separation of the bond has to be visually observed on the materials and on the adhesive film. The following kinds of failure can be evaluated:

·   Adhesion failure or detachment of the adhesive film from one of the materials
·   Cohesive failure or separation within the adhesive film without detachment from the material
·   Non-coalescence or failure of the two adhesive films to combine without detachment from the material
·   Breakdown of material of low structural strength at its surface
·   Partial or complete breakdown of material

The adhesives, the materials to be bonded to, and the bonding conditions may also be tested on footwear during production. Sole adhesion on the shoe can be tested by clamping shoe and sole on a tensile machine. Adhesion at the toe can be checked on the SATRA adhesion tester (STD 185).

5.5   Testing other shoe components

A shoe being an assembling of various components, each of them plays its role in the overall quality, and failure of one of them may spoil the performance of the shoe.

During the last decades, the development of new materials and new manufacturing technologies precipitated the development of new materials for insoles, toe puffs and stiffeners, linings and sockings, and fastening systems (54) with better comfort and performances.

Beside protection of the foot, comfort remains the main requirement for insoles and is evaluated by water vapour absorption/desorption (IUP 30 and EEC B1-B2). Combinations of cellulose board and non-woven or foam meet comfort and protection requirements.

Toe puffs and stiffeners have the greatest impact on the initial shape and the shape stability in use. Important properties are resilience (the ability of materials to retain their strength when repeatedly collapsed) and resistance to moisture.

Linings should provide comfort, measured by water vapour absorption and transmission (IUP 15 and 30, SATRA PA test), they should be light and flexible and keep those properties during wear. Shock absorption, cushioning and ground insulation are needed for sockings, inlays or inserts and washability is needed for sports footwear.

Fasteners, including laces, zips, elastics, touch-and-close materials are an important part of the quality image of footwear. Laces can be tested by AFNOR NF G 62020, touch-and-close materials by AFNOR NF G 62021 and zips by AFNOR NF G 91.

5.6 **Using computers for quality control in the leather and footwear industries** (55)

When evaluating materials used in footwear manufacturing and products in relation to their quality, a number of properties measured by different dimensions should be taken into consideration and not even all these parameters can be expressed in numerical terms.

A new system, which is built on the mathematical basis of scaling theory and cluster analysis (numerical taxonomy), is proposed. The main feature of the system is the objective manner of handling various properties simultaneously, while the process of product evaluation is based on mathematical computations. The results are produced in the form of ranked or preference lists, as well as in the form of groups (categories). The practical implementation is supported by computer programs (CITAX) to be run on personal computers. It can be applied in production management.

6.   ISO 9000

ISO 9000 is an international quality assurance system in design/development, production, installation and servicing. It is intended to lead to improved products and services. The ISO 9000 series (annex 1) meet the growing needs for international standardization in the quality arena and provide procedures for monitoring and controlling production or activities, ensuring that work is completed to agreed specifications or requirements and that problems are investigated and corrected. It introduces a philosophy of working for continual improvement and increased customer satisfaction.

To be effective, the system must be part of the company strategy, involving everyone from top management down. Managers and supervisors must be committed to improving the system, to accepting agreed procedures and promoting collaborative styles of working.

Quality is defined as the totality of features and characteristics of a product or service that bear on its ability to satisfy stated or implied needs, specified by the customer or identified and defined by the producer.

In many instances, needs can change with time.   This implies periodic revision of specifications. Needs may include aspects of usability, safety, reliability, maintainability, economics and environment.

The ISO 9000 standards deal with design and development (ISO 9001), purchasing, selling and contracts, all stages of the production including packaging (ISO 9002), final control and testing (ISO 9003). The last edition is dated April 1994.

The 20 requirements of ISO 9002 are as follows:

- Management responsibility: quality intentions and direction as formally expressed by top management and all aspects of quality management determining and implementing the quality policy
- Quality system: organizational structure, responsibilities, procedures, processes and resources for implementing quality management
- Contract review
- Design control
- Document and data control
- Purchasing
- Control of customer supplied product
- Product identification and traceability
- Process control
- Inspection and testing
- Control of inspection, measuring and test equipment
- Inspection and test status
- Control of nonconforming product
- Corrective and preventive action
- Handling, storage, packaging, preservation and delivery
- Control of quality records
- Internal quality audits
- Training
- Servicing
- Statistical techniques

The establishment of a quality system supposes extensive preparatory work and training of management and personnel. The procedure for obtaining ISO certification involves consultation of third-party bodies operating quality system registration programmes including auditing (56).

The ISO 9000 series introduces the procedure for a third-party certification scheme for quality systems registration, and for auditing compliance with the requirements.

Under such certification schemes, a company arranges to be audited by a single accredited independent (third-party) registrar organization. If the company's quality systems documentation and implementation are found to meet the requirements of the applicable ISO 9000 series standard, the registrar grants certification and lists the company in its register of companies with certified quality systems. All purchasers of the company's products can then accept the third-party certification as evidence that the company's quality systems meet the applicable ISO 9000 series requirements.

In addition to the certification, the benefits of the system are improvement in quality capability with reduction of poor or bad performance, of customer complaints or rejects, of repair or accidents, together with improvement of production and services.

To facilitate the understanding and implementation of the standards, ITC has published, in collaboration with ISO, a guide entitled "ISO 9000 quality management systems, guidelines for entreprises in developing countries". (57).

7. Recommended quality requirements

7.1 For leathers

7.1.1 GERIC-EURIS guidelines for leather
7.1.2 Quality requirements for garment leather (WGR)
7.1.3. Quality requirements for furniture leather (WGR)
7.1.4 Quality requirements for upholstered furniture leather
7.1.5. Quality requirements for bookbinding leather
7.1.6 TNO Recommendations
7.1.7 UNIDO guidelines

7.2 For footwear materials other than leather

7.2.1 Cotton lining materials (TNO Guidelines)

7.2.2 Antislip linings (TNO Guidelines)

7.2.3 Insole materials (non-leather)

7.2.4 Soling materials (non-leather)

7.3 Hidden quality requirements

7.1 For leathers

7.1.1 *GERIC-EURIS guidelines for leathers*

SHOE UPPER LEATHERS

Distension of grain	ISO/3379-IUP 9	min 7.00 mm
Tearing load	ISO/3377-IUP 8	
	For lined footwear	min 35 N*
	For unlined footwear	min 50 N
		max tear strength and thickness should be mentioned
Temperature resistance, fastness to ironing	IUF 458	min 80°C**
Patent leather after 3 min blowing at 100°C on leather distended on the lastometer or plastometer		no cracks
Finish adhesion	IUF 470-ISO 11644	
	Slightly corrected grain leather	dry min 3.0 N/cm wet min 2.0 N/cm
	Corrected grain leather	dry min 5.0 N/cm wet min 3.0 N/cm
	Light and fashion leathers (boxcalf, chevreau, sheep)	min 2.0 N/cm
	Patent leather	dry min 4.0 N/cm wet min 2.0 N/cm
	Coated leather	dry min 10.0 N/cm wet min 10.0 N/cm

*   For values under 35 N, reinforcing lining is recommended.

**   Hot air blowing should replace ironing if finish is not fast under 140°C.

Flexing endurance

IUP 20

Upper leathers	dry min 50,000 flx
	wet min 10,000 flx
Patent leather	dry min 20,000 flx
	wet min 10,000 flx

Rub fastness

IUF 450-ISO 11640

Casual shoes	min 50 motion
Unlined footwear on fleshside with	
Dry felt	min 50 motion
Wet felt	min 50 motion
Alkaline perspiration pH 9	min 50 motion
	staining of felt below grey scale 4
Fashion leathers	
Wet felt, dry leather	min 20 motion
Felt with water polish dry leather	min 20 motion
Dry felt, dry leather	min 50 motion

Substances soluble in dichloromethane (fat)

IUC 4

If one component adhesive	max 9%
If two component adhesive	max 14%
PU adhesive recommended if	more than 14%
For vulcanisation	max 8%
For PVC injection	max 15%

Water vapour absorption

After 8 hours	10 mg/cm2

on request

Tensile strength

ISO 3376 - IUP 6

(recommended for suede split)	min 150 N abs.
Elongation at break	not under 40%

Water resistance (penetrometer)	IUP 10 (for waterproof leather)	
	No water penetration	before 120 min
	Water absorption after 120 min	max 25%
Water vapour permeability*	IUP 15	
	Grain leather	1 mg/h.cm^2
	Corrected grain	0.8 mg/h.cm^2
Light fastness	IUF 401 (daylight) or IUF 402 (Xenon)	
	Blue scale	not below 3
pH of aqueous extract	ISO 4045 - IUP 11	not below 3.5
Water solubles	IUC 6	max 1.5 %
Water spotting fastness	IUF 420	no staining
Tensometer	At 18% linear extension	no grain crack

LINING LEATHERS

Rub fastness	ISO 11640 - IUF 450	
	Dry leather, wet felt	min 100 motions
	Dry leather, wet felt	min 50 motions
	Wet leather, dry felt	min 20 motions
	Dry leather, wet felt with alkaline perspiration pH 9	min 20 motions
	Dry leather with benzine-wetted felt	min 20 motions

*Not applicable to patent and coated leather

36

Migration test	
Staining of felt (on aniline leather)	not under 3 (grey scale)
Staining of felt (on pigmented leather)	not under 4
Annex 7 after 2 and 8 hours	no staining at contact surface higher than grey scale 3
Water vapour permeability	
IUP 15	min 1.0 mg/h.cm^2
Elongation at break	
IUP 6 (for leathers under 0.4 mm)	
Unlined skivers	min 25%
Lined skivers	min 30%
Other leathers	min 30%
Mineral water solubles	
IUC 6	max 1.5%
pH of aqueous extract	
ISO 4045 - IUC 11	not below 3.5
Solubles in dichloromethane (fat)	
Lining leathers	max 10%
Sheep wool linings	max 8%
On request	
Tearing load	
Reinforcement linings	min 15 N abs

LEATHER FOR INSOLES

		Vegetable-tanned	**Flexible split leather**
Water solubles	IUC 6		
	Total solubles	max 15%	max 6%
	Organic solubles	max 13%	max 4%
	Mineral solubles	max 2%	max 2%
pH of aqueous extract	ISO 4045		
	IUC 11	not below 3	not below 3.5
		under pH 4 difference figure max 0.7	under pH 4 difference figure max 0.7
Stitch tear		min 800 N/cm	min 650 N/cm
Migration test	Annex 7	no staining after 2 and 8 h.	no staining after 2 and 8 h.
On request			
Water absorption	IUP 7	after 8 hours min 35%	
Water desorption		after 16 hours min 40% of absorbed water	after 16 hours min 40% of absorbed water
Water vapour absorption		min 20 mg/cm^2/8 hours	min 20 mg/cm^2/8 hours

SOLE LEATHERS

Water solubles	IUC 6	
	Total solubles	max 20%
	Organic solubles	max 18%
	Mineral solubles	max 2%
Magnesium sulphate	ISO 5399 IUC 9	max 3% $MgSO_4 7H_2O$
Migration test	Annex 7	no staining
Waterproofness (permeometer)	IUP 11	
	Water penetration	after 20 min max 30%
	Water absorption	after 30 min max 30%
Water absorption	IUP 7	
	After 2 hours	max 35%
	After 24 hours	max 45%
On request		
pH of aqueous extract	IUC 11	not below 3
		if below 4, difference
		figure max 0.7
Tensile strength	IUP 6	min 2,250 N/cm^2

7.1.2 *Quality requirements for garment leathers*

Westdeutsche Gerberschule Reutlingen (58)

			Suede leathers, nubuck, nappa aniline	Nappa with finish
Light fastness	IUF 402	Wool blue scale	min 3	min 4
Rub fastness	IUF 450	Felt dry	20 motions	50 motions
		Felt wet	10 motions	20 motions
		Felt with alkaline perspiration	10 motions	20 motions
			Colour transfer to felt not below 3 on grey scale. Finished and nappa effect leathers should not exhibit any destruction of top cover.	
Flexing endurance	IUP 20		Nappa effect min 20.000 fx	min 50.000 fx
Finish adhesion	IUF 470		-	min 2 N/cm
Tear resistance	slit tear		min 150 N/cm	min 200 N/cm
Lamb leather				min 150 N/cm

Water penetration	IUF 420-time for penetration of	min 10 min
	a water drop	min 5 min
		no permanent staining after drying
Dyeing		Garment leathers should show deep colour penetration. The colour of the cross section must match the colour of the surface unless a colour contrast is aimed at for fashion effect.
pH of aqueous extract	IUC 11	not below 3.5
		not below 3.5
On request		
Tensile strength	IUP 6	min 1200 N/cm²
		min 1200 N/cm²
Dry cleaning fastness		after cleaning and rewaxing no change in feel, colour change not below 3–4 on grey scale, area change max 3%

7.1.3 *Quality requirements for furniture leathers*

Westdeutsche Gerberschule Reutlingen (59)

			Natural leather	Grain leather
Light fastness		IUF 402	min 3 on blue scale	
			for white leathers, no yellowing after 3 days storing at 50°C in the dark.	
Rub fastness		IUF 450		
	Dry felt		min 50 motions	min 500 motions
	Wet felt		min 20 motions	min 80 motions
	Felt with alkaline perspiration		min 20 motions	min 50 motions
	Staining of felt grey scale		min 3	min 4
Flexing endurance		IUP 20	-	min 20.000 fx
Finish adhesion		IUF 470	-	min 2 N/cm
Tearing load		DIN 53329	min 20 N/1 mm leather thickness	
pH of aqueous extract		IUC 11	min 3.5	
Dyeing			the colour of the cross-section must match the colour of the surface unless contrast is aimed at for fashion effect.	

7.1.4 Quality requirements for upholstered furniture leather: British Standard BS 7176.

7.1.5 Quality requirements for bookbinding leathers. British Standard BS 7451 specifies the chemical and physical properties of bookbinding leather where the main concerns are long-term resistance to pollution. The data used to prepare the standard were drawn from both natural ageing and accelerated laboratory tests. The standard contains tables listing the requirements for chrome, aluminium, pH and resistance to tarnishing and physical properties. It also covers approved marking. Methods for resistance to tarnishing and surface shrinkage are given in appendices.

7.1.6 TNO recommendations (additional to GERIC guidelines)

UPPER LEATHERS

Tensile strength	IUP 6	Side leathers	min 20 N/mm^2
		Sheepskin	min 12 N/mm^2
		Goatskin	min 15 N/mm^2
		Pigskin	min 20 N/mm^2
Tearing load	IUP 8	for safety and children shoes	min 100 N abs
Mineral water solubles	IUC 6		max 1.5%
Fat	IUC 4		max 10%
Heat resistance for vulcanization and injection	IUP 18		max loss in tensile strength and elongation at break 30%

LINING LEATHERS

Tearing load	IUP 8	min 30 N abs
Heat resistance for vulcanization and injection	IUP 18	max loss in tensile strength and elongation 30%

INSOLE LEATHERS

Tensile strength (parallel to backbone)	IUP 6		min 20 N/mm^2
Stitch tear	DIN 53333		min 65 N/mm
Behaviour against water	EEC B1	linear extension max 3%	
Water absorption	EEC B1-IUP 7		
	after 8 h		min 50%
	after 2 h		min 35%
Shape stability	IUP 30		
	linear contraction by drying from 65% R.H. to 45% R.H.		max 1%
	linear extension by humidifying from 65% to ± 100% R.H.		max 3%
Heat resistance for vulcanization and injection	IUP 17	linear contraction max 1% material should not become hard or brittle in the applied vulcanization or injection conditions.	

SOLING LEATHERS

Abrasion resistance	DIN 53516	max 300 mm^3
Fat	IUC 4	max 3%

7.1.7 UNIDO guidelines

	IUC		1	2	3	4	5	6	7	8	9	10	11	12	13	14
Mineral solubles	IUC 6	max %	2.0	2.0	2.0	2.0	2.0	2.0	1.0	2.0	3.0	2.5	2.0	2.0	2.0	2.0
$MgSO_4 \cdot 7H_2O$	IUC 9	max %	-	-	-	-	-	-	-	-	4.0	4.0	-	-	-	-
Cr_2O_3	IUC 8	min %	2.5	2.5	2.5	2.5	0.5	2.5	-	2.5	-	-	0.8	-	0.5	2.5
Fat	IUC 4	%	2-6	-	-	4-8	15-25	8-15	15-25	2-6	-	-	-	3-12	3-12	3-6
		max %	-	-	-	-	-	-	-	-	3.0	4.0	4.0	-	-	-
		min %	-	2.0	2.0	-	-	-	-	-	-	-	-	-	-	-
Water solubles	IUC 6	max %	-	-	-	-	6.0	-	6.0	6 - 10	16.0	10.0	10.0	6.0	3.0	-
pH of aqueous extract	IUC 11		Not below 3.5 Below 4.0, difference figure max 0.7													
PCP In the EU		ppm max	in all types of leather 1,000													
In Germany		ppm max	in all types of leather 5													

1 = calf leather
2 = side upper leather
3 = corrected grain
4 = goat
5 = retanned side upper leather
6 = waterproof chrome
7 = vegetable upper leather
8 = sole leather flexible
9 = sole leather
10 = insole leather
11 = combined tannage
12 = lining (vegetable)
13 = lining retanned
14 = lining chrome

UNIDO guidelines			1	2	3	4	5	6	7	8	9	10	11	12	13	14
Tensile strength	IUP 6	N/mm^2	20	20	20	20	25	30	25	20	20	20	10	15	15	15
Stitch tear	DIN 53333	N/mm	80	100	80	60	100	120	100	80	100	100	100	40	40	40
Tearing load	IUP 8	N/mm	30	40	25	40	40	40								
Water absorption after 2 h.	IUP 7	max %	60	60	60	60	30	30	35	40	40					
		min %	-	-	-	-	-	-	-	-	-	25	100	100	100	100
after 24 h.		max %	85	85	85	85	45	45	45	50	50	-	-	-	-	-
Apparent density	IUP 5	g/cm^3	-	-	-	-	-	-	-	-	1.15	1.05	1.0	-	-	-
Water vapour permeability	IUP 15	mg/cm^2/ h	250	250	250	250	180	200	200	250	200	200	250	300	300	300

1 = calf leather
2 = side upper leather
3 = corrected grain
4 = goat
5 = retanned side upper leather
6 = waterproof chrome
7 = vegetable upper leather

8 = sole leather flexible
9 = sole leather
10 = insole leather
11 = combined tannage
12 = lining (vegetable)
13 = lining retanned
14 = lining chrome

UNIDO guidelines

			Upholstery leather				Garment leather					Technical and other leathers					
			1	2	3	4	5	6	7	8	9	10	11	12	13	14	15
Mineral solubles	IUC 6	max %	2.0	2.0	2.0	2.0	2.0	2.0	2.0	8.0	2.0	2.0	2.0	2.0	1.5	5.0	6.0
Al$_2$O$_3$	IUC 16	min %	-	-	-	-	-	-	-	2.0	-	-	-	-	-	-	1.0
Cr$_2$O$_3$	IUC 8	min %	-	0.8	2.5	-	2.5	2.5	-	-	-	2.5	2.5	3.0	-	-	-
Fat	IUC 4	%	3 - 12	3 - 12	3 - 12	3 - 8	4 - 10	4 - 10	10	3 - 8	10-25	10-25	4 - 10	4 - 15	-	10	35
Water solubles	IUC 6	max %	6.0	6.0	-	6.0	-	-	-	4.0	6.0	-	-	-	-	-	-
pH of aqueous extract difference figure	IUC 11		Not below 3.5 Below 4.0, difference max. 0.7														

1 = vegetable-tanned
2 = retanned leather
3 = chrome-tanned
4 = cordovan-leather
5 = chrome-tanned
6 = glove leather (chrome)
7 = glove leather (alum)
8 = hat leather
9 = belt leather (vegetable)
10= belt leather
11 = football leather
12 = safety gloves leather
13 = parchment
14 = chamois
15 = oil-tanned (alum)

UNIDO guidelines			Upholstery leather				Garment leather				Technical and other leathers						
			1	2	3	4	5	6	7	8	9	10	11	12	13	14	15
Tensile strength	IUP 6	N/mm	-	-	-	10	10	10	10	10	25	25	30	15	50	10	10
	above	2 mm	25	25	25	-	-	-	-	-	-	-	-	-	-	-	-
	below	2 mm	10	10	15	-	-	-	-	-	-	-	-	-	-	-	-
Stitch tear	DIN 53333	N/mm	-	-	50	50	50	50	50	-	100	100	120	50	-	50	-
	above	2 mm	100	100	-	-	-	-	-	-	-	-	-	-	-	-	-
	below	2 mm	30	30	-	-	-	-	-	-	-	-	-	-	-	-	-
Tearing load	IUP 8	N/mm	-	-	20	20	15	15	20	-	40	40	40	30	-	15	-
	above	2 mm	40	40	-	-	-	-	-	-	-	-	-	-	-	-	-
	below	2 mm	15	15	-	-	-	-	-	-	-	-	-	-	-	-	-
Water absorption	IUP 7	max %	-	-	-	-					-	-	25	-	-	-	-
		min %	-	-	-	-					-	-	-	-	-	-	400

1 = vegetable-tanned
2 = retanned leather
3 = chrome-tanned
4 = cordovan leather
5 = chrome-tanned

6 = glove leather (chrome)
7 = glove leather (alum)
8 = hat leather
9 = belt leather (vegetable)
10= belt leather

11 = football leather
12 = safety gloves leather
13 = parchment
14 = chamois
15 = oil tanned (alum)

7.2 For footwear materials other than leather

7.2.1 Cotton lining material (TNO guidelines)

Property	Method	Unit	Value
Tearing load	TNO 3361	N min	20
Tensile strength	ISO 5081	N/mm min	8
Elongation at break Weft Warp		% min % min	 7 13
Water solubles	IUC 6 at 35°	% max	2 for sensitive leathers (aniline, light colours) 4 for other leathers
Abrasion (Martindale)	SATRA PM 31	number of revolutions	high grade medium grade

high grade dry 4000 / wet 2000
medium grade dry 2000 / wet 1000

7.2.2 Antislip lining (TNO guidelines)

Property	Method	Unit	Value
Tearing load	IUP 8	N min	30
Surface water absorption	TNO F42	mg/cm^2 min	30 after 15 minutes
Friction coefficient	TNO F5	min	0.50
Abrasion	SATRA PM 31		same as for cotton lining

7.2.3 *Insole materials (non-leather)*

TNO guidelines

			Grade 1	Grade 2	Grade 3
Tensile strength	IUP 6	N/mm² dry min	12	8	5
		wet min	8	5	3
Stitch tear	DIN 5331	N/mm dry min	50	40	25
		wet min	30	20	15
Elongation at break in cutting direction	IUP 6	%	15-40	15-40	15-40
Water resistance linear extension	EEC B1	% max	3	4	4
				No splitting in cross-section	
Water absorption	EEC B1	% min	50	40	30
		g/dm² min	6.5		
Shape stability	IUP 30				
Linear contraction by drying from 65% to 45% RH		% max	1	1	1
Linear extension by humidifying from 65% to ±100 RH		% max	3	4	4
Abrasion dry and wet	EEC B2	number of motions	1,000	750	5 0 0
Flexing endurance	TNO F4	min	1,000 flexes		

Property	Method	Unit				
Perspiration resistance linear contraction	TNO F1	% max	4	6	6	
				may not become brittle or hard		
Shear strength	EEC A5	N/mm² dry min wet min	1.5 1.2	1.2 1.2	1.2 1.0	
Heat resistance for vulcanization and injection, linear contraction vulcanisation or injection	IUP 17	% max		1.0		
				material should not become hard or brittle in the applied conditions.		

PFI guidelines

Property	Method	Unit		Value
Water absorption	IUP 7	after 8 h %	min	35
Water desorption		after 16 h.	min	40% of absorbed water
Swelling	IUP 30	%	max	20
Shape stability	IUP 30 Linear extension Linear contraction	% max % max		3 3
Abrasion	EEC B2 Dry min Wet min	number of motions		2,000 1,000
Mineral water solubles	IUC 6	% max		2
Tensile strength	IUP 6	N/mm² min		4
pH of aqueous extract	IUC 11			not below 3.5

7.2.4 *Soling materials (non-leather)*

ISO specifications. ISO 6907 gives requirements for two grades of resin rubber and hard rubber soling materials for soling without a heavy pattern: grade 1 (men's footwear) and grade 2 (boy's, girl's and women's footwear, footwear for light use, such as indoor footwear, including slippers).

Property	Test method			Grade 1	Grade 2
Density	ISO 2781	Mg/m^3	max	1.35	1.45
Hardness	ISO 48	IRHD	min	88	93
Tensile strength in both directions	ISO 37	MPa	min	7.5	6.5
Elongation at break in both directions	ISO 37	%	min	175	150
Cut growth in both directions at -5±2°C	ISO 6907, annex	kilocycles		100	50

51

TNO guidelines

Compact rubbers

				Grade 1	Grade 2	Grade 3
Density	ISO 2781	g/cm³	max	1.35	1.35	1.50
Hardness	EEC G3	Shore A		60-70	60-88	max 93
Tensile strength	EEC G2	N/mm²	min	8.0	7.0	5.5
Elongation at break		%	min	200	200	150
Tearing load	EEC G5	N/mm	min	10	8	6
Abrasion resistance	DIN 53516	mm³	max	150	200	300
Flexing endurance cut growth	DIN 53543	mm	max	6	8	10
Oil and benzine resistance swelling in iso-octane	ISO 1817	%	max	12	12	12

PVC

				Grade 1	Grade 2	Grade 3
Density	ISO 2781	g/cm³		1.18-1.27	1.18-1.27	1.18-1.27
Hardness	EEC G3	Shore A		58-74	58-74	58-74
Tensile strength	EEC G2	N/mm²		8-14	8-14	8-14
Elongation at break		%	min	300	300	300
Tearing load	EEC G5	N/mm	min	10	8	8

Property	Standard	Unit				
Abrasion resistance	ISO 53516	mm³	max	100	125	150
Flexing endurance cut growth at 20°C (on request at -5°C)	DIN 53543	mm	max	6	8	10
Poro-elastomers						
Density (for EVA)	ISO 2781	g/cm³	min	0.50 0.35	0.50 0.35	0.50 0.35
Tensile strength	EEC G2	N/mm²	min	3	2	2
Elongation at break		%	min	200	250	250
Tearing load	EEC G5	N/mm	min	3	2	2
Abrasion under 5 N load	DIN 53516	mm³	max	200	300	500
Linear contraction	EEC-G6	%	max	3.0	4.0	4.0
Flexing endurance cut growth	DIN 53543	mm	max	6	8	10
Thermoplastic rubbers						
Density	ISO 2781	g/cm³	min	1.10	1.10	1.10
Hardness	EEC G3	Shore A		60-80	60-80	60-80
Tensile strength	EEC G2	N/mm²	min	7.0	7.0	7.0
Elongation at break		%	min	300	300	300

	Standard	Unit				
Tearing load	EEC G5	N/mm	min	10	10	10
Abrasion	DIN 53516	mm³	max	180	180	180
Flexing endurance cut growth	DIN 53543	mm	max	6	8	10
Hard cellular rubber						
Density	ISO 2781	g/cm³	max	1.35	1.50	1.50
Hardness	EEC G3	Shore A	max	93	93	93
Tensile strength	EEC G2	N/mm²	min	7.0	6.0	5.0
Elongation at break		%	min	250	200	200
Tearing load	EEC G5	N/mm	min	8	6	6
Abrasion	DIN 53516	mm³	max	300	400	500
Flexing endurance cut growth	DIN 53543	mm	max	6	8	10
Flexible polyurethane						
Density	ISO 2781	g/cm³	min	0.7	0.6	0.5
Hardness — With skin	EEC G3	Shore A		50-80	50-80	50-80
Hardness — Without skin				45-75	45-75	45-75
Abrasion under 10 N load	DIN 53516	mm	max	100	200	300

Rubber for mid-soles

						PVC	PU
Tearing load	EEC-G5	N/mm	min	8		8	8
Stitch tear	EEC-G4	N/mm	min	35		35	35

PFI guidelines

				Compact rubber	Cellular Soft	Cellular Hard	PVC	PU
Tensile strength		N/mm²	min	7.0	3.0	7.0	8.0	5.0
Elongation at break		%	min	200	200	200	300	400
Tearing load		N/mm	min	80	30	80	80-100	60-100
Parallel to surface		N/cm width	min		20			
Flexing endurance		flexes	min	35.000	35.000	35.000	35.000**	30.000
Cut growth		mm	max	8	8	8		4
Shear		N/cm width	min	30	25	30		
Abrasion		mm³	max	400*	400-500	400-500	350	350
Shape stability contraction		%	max		3	2		

*Under 5 N load

**Summer shoes at ± 20°C, casual shoes at - 5°C, winter shoes at -10°C.

7.3   **Hidden quality requirements**

In addition to quantifiable properties, leathers are characterized by a set of properties that are difficult to measure and can only be subjectively evaluated. Those organoleptic properties, such as softness, feel, gloss, touch, colour or shade, are subject to personal judgement.

For footwear and other leather products, fashion will introduce factors such as model, combination of colours, application of accessories; comfort will require subjective appreciations of fit, shape etc.

Quantifiable properties can be translated into specifications identified by numbers corresponding to units of strength or mechanical resistance (newtons, kgf), of composition (% of constituents), of fastness (time, grey scales etc.). The goods can then be classified as good, acceptable or bad. For most of the organoleptic properties, the evaluation of the goods will be restricted to good or bad.

It is obvious that a quality evaluation of leather and leather products needs to combine all the quality parameters, more importance being given to the subjective aspects of the evaluation.

ANNEX I

I S O STANDARDS

TC 176   03.120.10   **Quality Management and Quality Assurance**

ISO 8402:1994	Quality management and quality assurance - Vocabulary
ISO 9000-1:1994	Quality management and quality assurance standards - Part 1: Guidelines for selection and use
ISO 9000-2:1993	Quality management and quality assurance standards - Part 2 - Generic guidelines for application of ISO 9001, ISO 9002 and ISO 9003
ISO 9000-3:1991	Quality management and quality assurance standards - Part 3 - Guidelines for the application of ISO 9001 to the development, supply and maintenance of software.
ISO 9000-4:1993	Quality management and quality assurance standards - Part 4: Guide to dependability programme management
ISO 9001:1994	Quality systems - Model for quality assurance in design, development, production, installation and servicing Technical corrigendum 1:1995 to ISO 9001
ISO 9002:1994	Quality systems - Model for quality assurance in production, installation and servicing Technical corrigendum 1:1995 to ISO 9002
ISO 9003:1994	Quality systems - Model for quality assurance in final inspection and test Technical corrigendum 1:1994 to ISO 9003 Technical corrigendum 2:1995 to ISO 9003
ISO 9004-1:1994	Quality management and quality system elements - Part 1: Guidelines
ISO 9004-2:1991	Quality management and quality system elements - Part 2: Guidelines for services Technical corrigendum 1:1994 to ISO 9004-2:1991
ISO 9004-3:1993	Quality management and quality system elements - Part 3: Guidelines for processed materials

ISO 9004-4:1993	Quality management and quality system elements - Part 4: Guidelines for quality improvement Technical corrigendum 1:1994 to ISO 9004-4:1993
ISO 10005: 1995	Quality management - Guidelines for quality plans (formerly ISO/DIS 9004-5)
ISO 10007:1995	Quality management - Guidelines for configuration management
ISO 10011-1:1990	Guidelines for auditing quality systems - Part 1: Auditing
ISO 10011-2:1991	Guidelines for auditing quality systems - Part 2: Qualification criteria for quality systems auditors
ISO 10011-3:1991	Guidelines for auditing quality systems - Part 3: Management of audit programmes
ISO 10012-1:1992	Quality assurance requirements for measuring equipment - Part 1: Metrological confirmation system for measuring equipment
ISO 10013:1995	Guidelines for developing quality manuals

CASCO[1]	03.120.20	**Product and company certification. Conformity assessment**

ISO/IEC Guide 7:1994	Guidelines for drafting of standards suitable for use for conformity assessment
ISO/IEC Guide 22:1982	Information on manufacturer's declaration of conformity with standards or other technical specifications
ISO/IEC Guide 23:1982	Methods of indicating conformity with standards for third-party certification systems
ISO/IEC Guide 25:1990	General requirements for the competence of calibration and testing laboratories
ISO Guide 27:1983	Guidelines for corrective action to be taken by a certification body in the event of misuse of its mark of conformity
ISO/IEC Guide 28:1982	General rules for a model third-party certification system for products

---

[1]   CASCO   Committee on Conformity Assessment
        IEC   International Electrotechnical Commission

ISO Guide 39:1988   General requirements for the acceptance of inspection bodies

ISO/IEC Guide 40:1983 General requirements for the acceptance of inspection bodies

ISO/IEC Guide 42:1984 Guidelines for a step-by-step approach to an international certification system

ISO/IEC Guide 43:1984 Development and operation of laboratory proficiency testing

ISO/IEC Guide 44:1985 General rules for ISO or IEC international third-party certification schemes for products

ISO/IEC Guide 48:1986 Guidelines for third-party assessment and registration of a supplier's Quality System

ISO/IEC Guide 53:1988 An approach to the utilization of a supplier's quality system in third-party product certification

ISO/IEC Guide 56:1989 An approach to the review by a certification body of its own internal quality system

ISO/IEC Guide 57:1991 Guidelines for the presentation of inspection results

ISO/IEC Guide 58:1993 Calibration and testing laboratory accreditation systems General requirements for operation and recognition

ISO/IEC Guide 60:1994 Code of good practice for conformity assessment

ISO/IEC TR 13233:1995Information technology - Interpretation of accreditation requirements in ISO/IEC Guide 25 Accreditation of Information Technology and Telecommunications testing laboratories for software and protocol testing services

Information publications on:

QUALITY MANAGEMENT AND CONFORMITY ASSESSMENT

ISO News — six issues a year, updates on ISO standards, news on their implementation and related developments

ISO Standards Compendium — contains the International Standards and draft International Standards of ISO 9000

Directory of quality systems registration bodies

Directory of quality systems training bodies
Vision 2000 — A strategy for International Standards' implementation in the quality arena during the 1990s

Tools to promote standardization in developing economies

ISO Development Manuals — A leaflet which presents the eight manuals intended specifically for developing countries

ISO 9000 Quality Management Systems: Guidelines for enterprises in developing countries, produced jointly by ITC Export Quality Management programme and ISO

TC 120	59.140	**LEATHER**
	59.140.20	**Raw skins, hides and pelts**
	ISO 2820:1974	Leather - raw hides of cattle and horses - method of trim
	ISO 2821:1974	Leather - Raw hides of cattle and horses- preservation by stack salting
	59.140.30	**Leather and furs**
	ISO 2588:1985	Leather - sampling - number of items for a gross sample
	ISO draft	Leather - wet-blue chrome tanned hides - specification

This last method was drafted by the technical committee without consulting of the leather industry and trade which expressed fierce criticism, principally of the chrome content determination and specification, the fungicidal test, the grain tightness evaluation and the hide substance determination.

All the other ISO methods for leather testing will be replaced by methods of the International Union of Leather Technologists and Chemists Societies IULTCS.

TC 137   61.060   **Footwear**

Standards prepared by technical committee TC 137 cover a shoe size system known as Mondopoint.

ISO 3836:1978   Shoe sizes - system of width grading (for use in the Mondopoint system

ISO 9407:1991   Shoe sizes - Mondopoint System of sizing and marking (replaces ISO 2816:1973, ISO 3355:1975 and ISO 3844:1977)

TC 45

The standards prepared by technical committee TC 45 are for rubber and plastic footwear, except one standard for rubber soling material

ISO 6907:1994   Vulcanized resin rubber and vulcanized hard rubber soling material - specification

TC 125   19.020   **Testing conditions**

ISO 554:1976   Standard atmospheres for conditioning and/or for testing

ISO 558:1980   Conditioning and testing - standard atmosphere - definitions

ISO 3205:1976   Preferred test temperatures

ISO 4677:1985   Atmospheres for conditioning and testing - determination of relative humidity -
Part 1: Aspirated psychrometer method
Part 2: Whirling psychrometer method

TC 12   01.060   **Quantities and Units**

ISO 31-0:1992   Quantities and units - Part 0: General Principles

ISO 31-1:1992   Quantities and units - Part 1: space and time

ISO 31-2:1992   Quantities and units - Part 2: periodic and related phenomena

ISO 31-3:1992   Quantities and units - Part 3: mechanics

ISO 31-4:1992   Quantities and units - Part 4: heat

ISO 31-5:1992   Quantities and units - Part 5: electricity and magnetism

ISO 31-6:1992	Quantities and units - Part 6: light and related electromagnetic radiations
ISO 31-7:1992	Quantities and units - Part 7: acoustics
ISO 31-11:1992	Quantities and units - Part 11: mathematical signs and symbols for use in the physical sciences and technology
ISO 31-12:1992	Quantities and units - Part 12: characteristic numbers
ISO 1000:1992	SI units and recommendations for the use of their multiples and of certain other units

ENVIRONMENT

ISO Standards Compendium Environment

Water quality (3 volumes)

Air quality   (one volume)

Soil quality (one volume)

ANNEX II

IULTCS METHODS

IUP PHYSICAL TESTING METHODS

1.   IUP methods which will be converted to ISO

IUP 2	Sampling (ISO 2418)
IUP 3	Conditioning (ISO 2419)
IUP 4	Measurement of thickness (ISO 2589)
IUP 5	Measurement of apparent density (ISO 2420)
IUP 6	Measurement of

          (a) tensile strength

          (b) percentage of elongation caused by a specified load

          (c) percentage elongation at break (ISO 3376)

IUP 7	Measurement of absorption of water (ISO 2417)
IUP 8	Measurement of tearing load (ISO 3377)
IUP 9	Measurement of distension and strength of grain by the ball burst test (Lastometer)
IUP 10	Water resistance for flexible leathers (Penetrometer)
IUP 11	Dynamic waterproofness test for boot and shoe sole leather (Permeometer)
IUP 12	Measurement of resistance to grain cracking
IUP 15	Measurement of water vapour permeability
IUP 16	Measurement of shrinkage temperature (ISO 3380)
IUP 20	Measurement of the flexing endurance of light leathers and their surface finishes (Flexometer)
IUP 32	Area measurement (ISO 11646)
IUP 35	Heat resistance for industrial glove leathers (ISO 11645)

2.   IUP methods which will not be converted to ISO

IUP 13	Measurement of two-dimensional extension (Tensometer)
IUP 14	Measurement of the waterproofness of gloving leathers
IUP 17	Assessment of the resistance of air-dry insole leathers to heat with special reference to the direct moulded process of footwear construction
IUP 18	Assessment of the resistance of air-dry lining leathers to heat with special reference to the direct moulded process of footwear construction
IUP 19	Assessment of the resistance of air-dry upper leathers to heat with special reference to the direct moulded process of footwear construction
IUP 21	The measurement of set in lasting with the dome plasticity apparatus
IUP 24	Measurement of surface shrinkage by immersion in boiling water
IUP 26	Determination of the abrasion resistance of sole leather (draft)
IUP 29	Determination of cold crack resistance of finishes

IUP 30   Determination of water vapour absorption and desorption and related changes of dimensions of leather

IUP 33   Fogging test (draft)

3.   <u>IUP methods which were deleted</u>

IUP 22   The assessment of damage by use of the viewing box

IUP 23   The measurement of surface damage by an impact

IUP 28   Measurement of the resistance to bending of heavy leather

IUF FASTNESS TESTING METHODS

GROUP 1		General information, principles, assessment scales, preparation of standard substrates.	
	IUF 105	Numbering code for the Standard Methods of Test and Standards for Methods of Testing	(+)
	IUF 120	General principles of colour fastness testing of leather (based on ISO 105-A01)	to withdraw
	IUF 131	Grey scale for assessing change in colour - to be replaced by the ISO method	ISO 105A02
	IUF 132	Grey scale for assessing staining (to be replaced by the ISO method)	ISO 105A03
		Method for the instrumental assessment of the change in colour of a test specimen	ISO 105A05
		Method for defining the viewing conditions	ISO 105A07
	IUF 142	Artificial ageing	draft
	IUF 151	Preparation of storable standard chrome grain leather for dyeing	draft
Group 2		Testing the properties of dyestuffs and finishes without the aid of leather	
	IUF 201	Approximate determination of the solubility of leather dyes	in revision
	IUF 202	Fastness to acid of dye solutions	in revision
	IUF 203	Stability to acid of dye solutions	in revision
	IUF 204	Stability of dyes in solution to alkali	draft
	IUF 205	Stability to hardness of dye solutions	in revision
	IUF 207	Stability of dyes in solution to multivalent cationic electrolytes	draft
Group 3		Testing the properties of dyestuffs and finishing material without the aid of leather	
Group 4		Colour fastness testing of leather	
	IUF 401	Colour fastness of leather to light: daylight	ISO 105B01
	IUF 402	Colour fastness of leather to light: Xenon lamp	ISO 105B02

	Colour fastness of leather to artificial light at high temperature	ISO 105B06
IUF 420	Colour fastness of leather to water spotting	
IUF 421	Colour fastness of leather to water	ISO 11642
IUF 423	Colour fastness of leather to washing - mild washing	
IUF 424	Colour fastness of leather to formaldehyde	withdrawn
IUF 426	Colour fastness of leather to perspiration	ISO 11641
IUF 434	Colour fastness of small samples to dry cleaning solutions	ISO 11643
IUF 435	Fastness of leather to machine washing	
IUF 441	Colour fastness of leather in respect of staining raw crepe rubber	(++)
IUF 442	Colour fastness of leather in respect of staining plasticized polyvinyl chloride	
IUF 450	Colour fastness of leather to cycles of to-and-fro rubbing	ISO 11640
IUF 454	Colour fastness of leather to buffing	(+)
IUF 458	Colour fastness of leather to ironing	
IUF 470	Test for adhesion of finish	ISO 11644

(+) Methods which will not become ISO.

(++) Methods not currently used and will probably be withdrawn.

Method IUF 151 has been proposed to be replaced by the draft method VESLIC - C 1510 Sept.93,
Manufacture of standard full grain chrome leather.

New methods to be drafted:
- Method for preservation of wet chrome leather and chrome hide powder
- Oil resistance of leather
  An ASTM method will be drafted in ISO format and proposed as an IUF method

IUC CHEMICAL ANALYSIS METHODS

IUC 1	General instructions (expression of results)		
IUC 2	Sampling (laboratory samples - location and identification)	ISO	2418
IUC 3	Preparation of test material by grinding	ISO	4044
IUC 4	Determination of substances soluble in dichloromethane (fat)	ISO	4048
IUC 5	Determination of volatile matter (moisture)		
IUC 6	Determination of water-solubles, inorganic water-solubles and organic water-solubles		
IUC 7	Determination of total ash and water-insoluble ash (sulphated)	ISO	4047
IUC 8	Determination of chromic oxide (*)		
IUC 9	Determination of water-soluble magnesium salts (EDTA titrimetric method)	ISO	5399
IUC 10	Determination of Nitrogen and of "hide substance" (titrimetric method)	ISO	5397
IUC 11	Determination of pH and difference figure of an aqueous leather extract	ISO	4045
IUC 12	Determination of sulphur in leather		
IUC 13	Determination of zirconium in leather		
IUC 14	Determination of silicon in leather (reduced molybdosilicate spectrometric method)	ISO	5400
IUC 15	Determination of phosphorus in leather		
IUC 16	Determination of aluminium in leather (*)		
IUC 17	Determination of hydroxyproline		
IUC 18	Photometric determination of chromium (VI) using 1,5-diphenylcarbazide		
IUC 20	Determination of the proteolytic activity of enzymes		

Determination of titanium in leather
Determination of formaldehyde in leather
Determination of PCP in leather
Benzidine test

(*) in revision

ANNEX III

OTHER INTERNATIONAL STANDARDS

CEN and EUROPEAN STANDARDS

TC 200	SAFETY	Tannery machines and plant-safety
TC 201		Leather products machinery-safety
TC 289	LEATHER	

FEICA STANDARDS

Method A 1   Testing the bondability of shoe materials

Method A 2   Testing of adhesives for upper and bottom materials

Method A 3   EEC A3 -   Determination of the peel resistance of adhesive joints

Method A 4   EEC A4 -   Testing of adhesive joints - Creep test

Method A 5   EEC A5 -   Determination of the shear strength of adhesive joints

EURIS STANDARDS

EEC - B1   Testing behavior of footwear materials against water
EEC - B2   Determination of the rub resistance of the surface of insole and anti-slip materials

EEC - F1   Determination of colorfastness during storage in the dark

EEC - G   Testing of soling elastomers
EEC - G1   Preparation of test pieces
EEC - G2   Measurement of tensile strength and elongation at break
EEC - G3   Measurement of Shore A hardness
EEC - G4   Determination of stitch tear
EEC - G5   Determination of tear strength
EEC - G6   Determination of shrinkage

Institutes member of EURIS

Centro Tecnológico do Calçado
San Joao da Madeira
Portugal

CIMAC
Vigevano
Italy

C T C
Lyon

EL.KE.DE
Kallithea Athens

France

Greece

INESCOP
Elda Alicante
Spain

P F I
Pirmasens
Germany

SATRA
Kettering
England

ANNEX IV

SOME NATIONAL STANDARDS

PHYSICAL TESTING METHODS

Method	Official		Similar Methods				
	IU	ISO	AFNOR	ASTM	BS	DIN	VESLIC
Sampling	IUP 2	2418	G 52 000	D 2813	3144/1	53 302	E 3020
Conditioning	IUP 3	2419	G 52 001	D 1610-69		53 303	E 3050
Thickness	IUP 4	2589	G 52 010	D 1813	3144/3	53 326	E 3107
Apparent density	IUP 5	2420	G 52 011	D 2346-68	3144/4	53 327	E 3108
Tensile strength	IUP 6	3376	G 52 002	D2209/ 08/11	3144/5	53 328	E 3110
Water absorption	IUP 7	2417	G 52 009	D 1815-70	3144/18	53 330	E 3201
Tearing load	IUP 8	3377	G 52 014	D 1704 / D 2212-64	3144/6	53 329	E 3111
Lastometer	IUP 9	3379	G 52 007	D 2207-64	3144/8	53 325	
Penetrometer	IUP 10		G 52 015	D 2099 / D 2098-70	3144/21	53 338	E 3202
Permeometer	IUP 11				3144/22	53 338T2	E 3202
Grain cracking	IUP 12	3378	G 52 006		3144/7	53 324	
Water vapour permeability	IUP 15		G 52 013	D 5052	3144/24	53 333	
Shrinkage temperature	IUP 16	3880	G 52 012		3144/17	53 336	E 1112
Flexing endurance	IUP 20		G 52 018		3144/13	53 351	C 4700
Area measurement	IUP 32	11646					
Heat resistance	IUP 35	11645					
Surface shrinkage	IUP 24						
Abrasion, sole leather	IUP 26	3378				53 516	

FASTNESS TESTING METHODS

Method	Official				Similar Methods			
	IU	ISO	AFNOR	ASTM	BS	DIN	VESLIC
Grey scale fading	IUF 131	105A-02	G 07-011		1006-A02	54 001	C 1210
Grey scale staining	IUF 132	105A-03	G 07-011		1006-A03	54 002	C 1220
Fastness, daylight	IUF 401	105B-01			1006 B01		
Fastness, xenon	IUF 402	105B-02	G 52 302		1006 B02	54 004	C 4020
Fastness to water	IUF 421	11 642			1006		C 4230
Water spotting	IUF 420			D 1913	1006-13	53 888	
Fastness to washing	IUF 423			D 2096	1006-10		C 4250
Fastness to perspiration	IUF 426	11 641	G 52 304	D 2322			
Fastness to dry cleaning	IUF 434	11 643	G 52 303		7269 1-2		C 4340
Fastness to rubbing	IUF 450	11 640	G 52 301		1006-8	53 339	C 4500
Adhesion of finish	IUF 470	11 644					C 4800

LEATHER CHEMICAL ANALYSIS

Method	Official		Similar Methods					
	IU	ISO	AFNOR	ASTM	BS	DIN	VESLIC	
Sampling	IUC 2	2418	G 52 201			1309/1	53 302	
Grinding	IUC 3	4044	G 52 201	D 2813		1309/2	53 303	
In solvent soluble	IUC 4	4048	G 52 204	D 3495		1309/4	53 306	E 1160
Volatile matter	IUC 5		G 52 202	D 3790		1309/3	53 304	E 1121
Water solubles	IUC 6		G 52 205	D 2876		1309/5	53 307	E 1170
Total ash	IUC 7	4047	G 52 203	D 2617		1309/6	53 305	E 1122
Chromic oxide	IUC 8		G 52 208	D 2807		1309/8	53 309	E 1123
Magnesium sulphate	IUC 9	5399	G 52 217			1309/11	53 310	E 1125
Hide substance	IUC 10	5397	G 52 206	D 2668		1309/7	53 308	E 1150
pH and difference index	IUC 11	4045	G 52 214	D 2810		1309/9	53 312	E 1200
Silicon	IUC 14	5400	G 52 211			1309/12		
Aluminium	IUC 16		G 52 209					

NATIONAL STANDARDS FOR FOOTWEAR
and LEATHER ARTICLES

1. AFNOR[2]

NF G-60 001 to 60 003 **Mondopoint**

NF G-60 004	Arrière de forme pour chaussures de ville hommes, construction, contrôle, marquage
NF G-60 005	Pointures Mondopoint
NF G 62	*Méthodes d'essais*
NF G 62 001	Chaussures - Détermination de la résistance à l'abrasion des matériaux à semelle (cuirs et matériaux divers) utilisés dans l'assemblage de la chaussure
NF G 62 002	Chaussures - Détermination de la capacité d'absorption et de désorption d'eau des matériaux pour semelles premières
NF G 62 003	Chaussures - Essai d'imperméabilité du cuir à semelle
NF G 62 004	Chaussures - Détermintion de la pénétration d'eau dans les cuirs à dessus
NF G 62 005	Solidité des teintures au frottement translatif à l'état sec et humide
NF G 62 006	Chaussures - Semelles en caoutchouc et en matières plastiques - Détermination de la résistance à la rupture et de l'allongement à la rupture
NF G 62 010	Chaussures - Détermination de la résistance à la flexion répétée des matériaux à dessus
NF G 62 011	Chaussures - Détermination de la capacité d'isolation thermique des matériaux à dessus et à semellage
NF G 62 012	Chaussures - Détermination de l'adaptabilité de la tige
NF G 62 013	Chaussures - Détermination de la résistance des points d'arrêt
NF G 62 014	Chaussures - Détermination de la résistance au pelage de l'assemblage tige/semelle
NF G 62 020	Chaussures - Détermination de la résistance des lacets et de l'effet tranchant des accessoires de passage
NF G 62 021	Chaussures - Détermination de la tenue de l'accrochage des rubans auto-agrippants
NF G 83 001	Machines pour chaussures - Couteau circulaire pour machine à parer les peaux
NF G 90	*Machines à coudre*
NF G 91	Fermetures à glissière
NF G 92	Bagagerie

2. British Standards

BS	Methods of test for leather (see Annex 4)
BS 5131	Methods of test for footwear and footwear materials
	Part 1. *Adhesives*

Many AFNOR standards are available in the English language

Section 1.1.   *Resistance of adhesive joints to heat (creep test)*
Method for measuring the resistance of an adhesive joint when subjected to a constant peeling force at a controlled elevated temperature over a timed interval.

Section 1.2.   *Resistance of adhesive joints to peeling*
Method for measuring the resistance of an adhesive joint when subjected to peeling at a constant rate of separation.

Section 1.3.   *Preparation of test assemblies using adhesives (other than hot melt adhesives) for heat resistance (creep) and peel tests*
Methods for preparation of test assemblies.

Section 1.4.   *Heat activation life of adhesives*

Section 1.6.   *Recommended environmental storage conditions for adhesive joints prior to heat resistance or peeling tests*

Section 1.7.   *The preparation of hot melt adhesive bonded assemblies for heat resistance and peel tests*

Section 1.8.   *Rate of bond strength development in shear of hot melt adhesives for lasting*

Section 1.9.   *Measurement of green strength of adhesive joints*

BS 5350   Methods of test for adhesives

Part B2   *Determination of solids content*
Part B4   *Method for the determination of the working life of an adhesive using viscosity tests, bond strength or both. (pot life)*

Part B8   *Determination of viscosity*
Part C10   *90 °peel test for a flexible-to-rigid assembly*

BS 5350   Physical tests on hot melt adhesives

Part H1   *Determination of heat stability of hot melt adhesives in the application equipment*
Part H2   *Determination of low temperature flexibility or cold crack temperature*
Part H3   *Determination of heat resistance of hot melt adhesives*
Part H4   *Determination of maximum open time of hot melt adhesives (oven method)*

Part 2. *Solings*

Section 2.1.   *Ross flexing method for cut growth resistance of soling materials*
Section 2.6.   *Split tear strength of cellular solings*

Section 2.7. *The preparation of test pieces from soling materials for physical testing*

Section 2.10. *Measurement of heat shrinkage of cellular solings*

Section 2.11. *Resistance of solings to short-term contact with a hot surface*

BS EN 344 Requirements and test methods for safety, protective and occupational footwear for professional use.

BS EN 345 Specification for <u>safety</u> footwear for professional use.

BS EN 346 Specification for <u>protective</u> footwear for professional use.

BS EN 347 Specification for <u>occupational</u> footwear for professional use.

BS 5833 Scheme for labeling of footwear

3. DIN standards

Leather group 53 (see annex IV)

DIN 53 313 E10-93 Determination of PCP in leather

Footwear

DIN 66074 *Shoe sizes; length grading*

DIN 66074 Part 1 *Shoe sizes; fundamental characteristics of Mondopoint*

Personal safety and protection

DIN 4843 *Safety devices for footwear*

DIN 4843 Part 1 *Safety footwear; construction, safety requirements and testing*

Part 2 *Safety footwear; construction, materials, testing*

Adhesives

DIN 53271 *Testing adhesives for soling; concept, preparation of test pieces*

DIN 53272 *Testing adhesives for soling; data on materials, adhesives and adhesion process*

DIN 53273 *Testing adhesives for soling; shear test*

DIN 53274 *Testing adhesives for soling; peel test*

Soling materials

DIN 53504 *Testing of elastomers - determination of tear strength, tensile strength, elongation at break*

DIN 53505 *Hardness, Shore A and D*

DIN 53506 *Determination of stitch tear*

DIN 53516 *Abrasion resistance*

DIN 53522 *Flexing endurance De Mattia*

ANNEX V

INTERNATIONAL CONTRACTS OF ICHSLTA AND ICT

By agreement between the International Council of Hides, Skins and Leather Traders' Associations (ICHSLTA) and the International Council of Tanners (ICT) international contracts were established to facilitate orderly trading and to provide protection to buyer and seller alike, particularly in respect of resolving disputes without recourse to expensive litigation.

The International Contract for Hides and Skins has been in use for more than 60 years. In accordance with changes in shipping methods and other situations the contracts have been constantly updated. The most recent versions are contracts 6 and 7, which came in force in May 1993. They replace contracts 4 and 5.

International Contract 6 covers:

   Raw hides and skins

   Pickled hides and skins, pickled grains and pickled splits

   Wet-blue hides and skins, wet-blue splits
   Chrome, vegetable or other tanned unfinished leather in the dry or crust condition.

International Contract 7 covers finished leather

ANNEX VI

SI UNITS

The SI unit system (Système International d'Unités) was adopted in 1960 and gradually introduced to virtually all countries. It is based on seven primary units:

Quantity	Unit	Symbol
Length	metre	m
Mass	kilogram	kg
Time	second	s
Electric current	ampere	A
Temperature	kelvin	K
Luminous intensity	candela	cd
Amount of substance	mole	mol

Decimal multiples and submultiples of SI units:

Prefix	Symbol	Factor	
tera	T	10^{12}	
giga	G	10^{9}	billion
mega	M	10^{6}	million
kilo	k	10^{3}	thousand
hecto	h	10^{2}	hundred
deca	da	10^{1}	ten
deci	d	10^{-1}	tenth
centi	c	10^{-2}	hundredth
milli	m	10^{-3}	thousandth
micro	u	10^{-6}	
nano	n	10^{-9}	
pico	p	10^{-12}	
femto	f	10^{-15}	
atto	a	10^{-18}	

For convenience, the Celsius scale is still accepted (symbol, °C), and minute (min), hour (h) and day (d) are accepted as multiples of the second.

The most common SI-derived units in material testing are the following:

- The **newton** is the force that applied to the mass of 1 kilogram, gives it an acceleration of 1 metre per second square.

- The **pascal** is the pressure produced by a force of 1 Newton applied, uniformly distributed, over an area of 1 square metre.

  The **joule** is the work done when the point of application of a force of 1 Newton is displaced through a distance of 1 metre in the direction of the force.

QUANTITY	NAME	SYMBOL	RELATIONSHIP
Force	newton	N	$1\,N = \dfrac{m\,kg}{sec^2}$
Pressure	pascal	Pa	$1\,Pa = \dfrac{1\,N}{m^2}$
Work, energy	joule	J	$1\,J = 1\,N\,m$

1 kgforce = 10 N = 1 daN

ANNEX VII

DRAFT METHOD FOR MEASUREMENT OF LEATHER SOFTNESS

1.   Introduction

This method describes a non-destructive means of assessing the softness of a leather. It is applicable to any light leather.

2.   Apparatus

The apparatus used shall be provided with the following parts:

2.1   A circular aperture selected from one of the following.

Nominal diameter (A) (mm)	Actual diameter (mm)
35	34.975±0.025
25	24.975±0.025
20	19.975±0.025

2.2   A clamp (B) for securely holding the leather sample whilst leaving the portion above the aperture free to move. The clamp shall hold the clamped area stationary when a force of 5.3 N is applied to the centre.

2.3   A cylindrical load pin (C) of diameter 4.89±0.10 mm and length 11.5±0.1 mm. The load pin is rigidly attached to the centre of a cylindrical mass (D). The total mass shall be 530±10 g.

2.4   A means of guiding the load pin such that it acts perpendicularly to the leather sample and restricts the vertical travel of the load pin to a distance of 11.5±1 mm.

2.5   A means of lowering the load pin onto the leather such that the load pin travels its full permitted distance of 11.5±0.1 mm in 1.5±0.5 seconds.

2.6   A gauge reading to 0.1 mm to directly measure the distension of the leather by the load pin.

2.7   A flat rigid metal disc of minimum diameter 60 mm for zeroing the gauge.

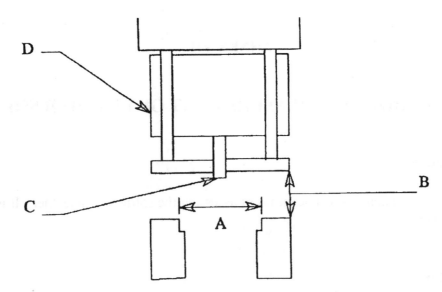

Cross-sectional view of the working head of the apparatus.

3. Preparation of sample

Condition the sample in accordance with IUP 3. The sample must be free from any obvious physical defects such as flay cuts in the area where softness is measured.

4. Procedure

4.1 Select the aperture to be used (see note 1).

4.2 Place the leather over the circular aperture, ensuring that the aperture is completely covered with sufficient sample for effective clamping.

4.3 Raise the load pin and clamp the leather in position.

4.4 Release the load pin and allow the reading in the gauge to become steady.

4.5 Record the deflection on the gauge.

4.6 To check that the instrument is reading zero, place the rigid metal plate on the lower clamp plate and follow the procedure in 4.3-4.5. This will give zero deflection and the gauge can be set accordingly.

5. Reporting

The report shall include

1. A reference to this method (i.e. IUP/XX)

2. The nominal diameter of the aperture

3.   The deflection recorded on the gauge in mm

4.   Details of the sample

Notes

1.   The following guidance is given for selection of the aperture:
35 mm, measurement of firmer leathers (e.g., shoe uppers);
25 mm, measurement of leathers of moderate softness (e.g. upholstery leathers); and
20 mm, measurement of softer leathers (e.g., gloving and light clothing leathers). These suggestions are only guidelines and best results for each individual case will be achieved with practice and experimentation.

2.   Depending on the final profile of the instrument, it may be possible to make measurement over the whole skin or side without cutting out a sample.

ANNEX VIII

MIGRATION TEST[3]

Test pieces of leather 20 mm x 40 mm are placed with the surface to be tested (grain or flesh side) in contact with longer strips of filter paper 20 mm x 100 mm in such a way that one end of the leather test piece remains free. A 15 mm leather piece and filter paper are clamped (e.g. with a wash clamp) between two glass plates (microscope glass slides). The composite test piece is dipped with one narrow edge in a glass dish containing demineralized water up to a height of 10 mm so that only the leather is in contact with the water and not the filter paper. The test is performed on multiple test pieces; after two hours and after additional increments of time, up to 8 hours, the filter papers are dried at room temperature and the coloration is evaluated with the grey scale for staining (IUF 132).

When the migration of salts (magnesium sulphate) is tested, the evaluation is easier on black filter paper.

The influence of perspiration can be evaluated by replacing the demineralized water by an artificial perspiration solution.

It is also possible to make a test piece by stitching or fixing together upper leather and sole leather with an overlapping of 10 mm. One edge of the sole leather is dipped into water that migrates into the upper leather; when the latter becomes wet, it is dried. Spew, discolouration or hardening can be observed.

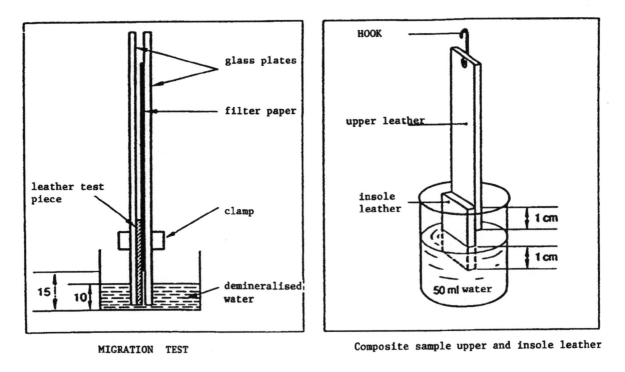

MIGRATION TEST   Composite sample upper and insole leather

Procedure and drawings are taken from "Qualitätsbeurteilung von Leder, Lederfehler, Lederlagerung and Lederpflege" J. Lange, (Bibliothek des Leders) pg.143-144. Also from "Werkstoffprüfung - Testmethoden und Verfahren", W. Fisher, W. Schmidt PSI Pirmasens y.

ANNEX IX

TESTING EQUIPMENT

1.   Cutting knives

The internal surfaces of each press knife shall be normal to the plane which contains the cutting edge. The angle formed at the cutting edge between the internal and external surfaces of the press knife shall be approximately 20 degrees, and the wedge of this angle shall be of a depth exceeding the thickness of the leather (figure 1).

The cutting knives can be made from steel straps used for making cutting dies in the footwear industry, except for heavy leathers for which forged dies are requested.

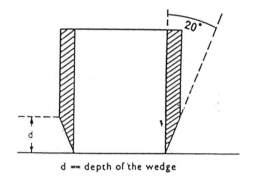

d = depth of the wedge

Figure 1. Shapes of press knives

To obtain cleanly cut test pieces, the cutting knives used must be sharp and clean, without splinters.

for   **IUP 5 apparent density, and IUP 7 water absorption,**
a circular knife of 70 mm diameter is used

for   **IUP 6 tensile strength,** the shape and dimensions of the internal surfaces of the press knife which must be used to cut the test piece are shown in figure 2

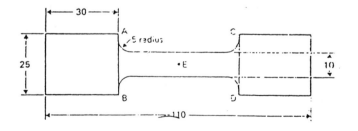

Figure 2

For heavy belting or sole leather, a larger specimen may be used.

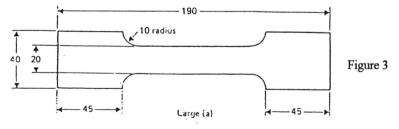

Figure 3

If only small samples of leather are available or if the test piece has to be cut in a shoe or a leather manufactured product, a small test piece may be used (figure 4). The thickness should then be measured before the leather is cut.

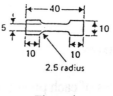

Figure 4

For **IUP 8, tearing load,** the specimen is a rectangle 50 mm long and 25 mm wide, in which a slot having the shape and dimensions shown in figure 5 has been cut, preferably by use of a press knife which cuts out the specimen and slot in one operation.

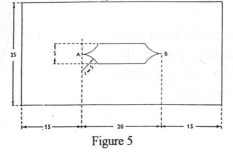

Figure 5

For the "Trouser" test pieces, size and shape are given in figure 6 for the French NF G 52-004 specimen and the two German DIN specimens.

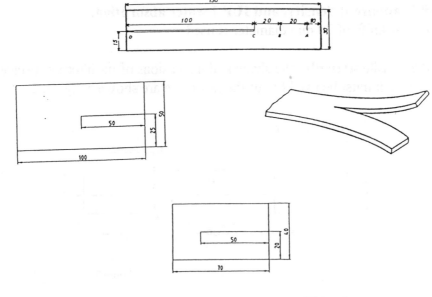

Figure 6

The stitch tear test needs a rectangular cutting knife 20 mm wide by at least 50 mm long

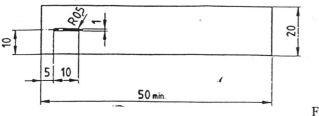

Figure 7

For **IUP 9 Lastometer** the cutting knife is a circle of 44.5 mm having at both ends of one diameter two indents allowing location of the test piece in the instrument.

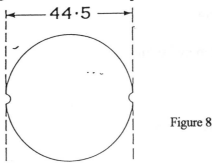

Figure 8

For the other tests:

IUP 10, Penetrometer, a rectangle of 75 mm by 60 mm

IUP 11, Permeometer, a rectangle of 100 mm by 40 mm

IUP 12, Grain cracking, a rectangle of 150 mm by 25 mm

IUP 13, Tensometer, a circle of 68 mm diameter

IUP 15, Water vapour permeability, the specimens are circles whose diameters are equal to the exterior diameters of the necks of the bottles placed in the apparatus (approximately 34 mm).

IUP 16, Shrinkage temperature, the specimen for leather thickness less then 3 mm is a rectangle 50 mm by 3mm, for leather thickness over 3 mm, a rectangle 50 mm by 2mm.

IUP 20, Flexometer

   a rectangle 70 mm by 45 mm

IUP 21, dome plasticity

   a circle of 90 mm diameter

IUP 24, surface shrinkage

   a circle of 70 mm diameter

IUP 27, water vapour absorption

a circle of 85 mm diameter

IUP 30, water vapour absorption/desorption

a square of 100 mm by 100 mm

IUF 423, mild washing
IUF 426, perspiration
IUF 434, dry cleaning
IUF 435, machine washing

a rectangle of 100 mm by 36 mm

IUF 424, formaldehyde

a rectangle 50 mm by 30 mm

IUF 450, rubbing
IUF 454, buffing
IUF 458, ironing

a rectangle of 120 mm by 50 mm

IUF 470, adhesion of finish

a rectangle of 100 mm x 10 mm

Tensile strength on elastomers

sample according to DIN 53 504

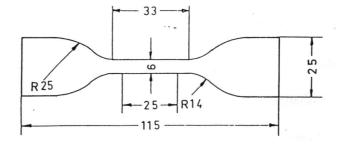

Fig. 9

For adhesive testing

a rectangle of 150 mm x 30 mm or 80 mm x 20 mm

2. Holders and special tools

For IUP 8, tearing load, specimen holders to attach to the jaws of the tensile machine are shown in figure 10. Each consists of a strip of steel 10 mm wide and 2 mm thick, bent through a right angle at one end and welded to a bar which makes the strip rigid and which fits or replaces one pair of jaws.

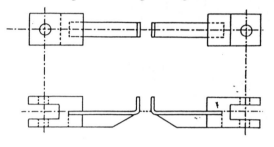

Figure 10

A simple pair of specimen holders can be made by screwing Alen keys in the axis of pieces which fit in the jaw of the machine.

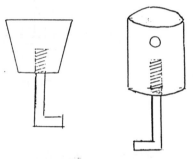

Figure 11

For the stitch tear, specimen holder in figure 12 is suggested for leather, the one in figure 13 is recommended for the needle stitch tear on elastomers.

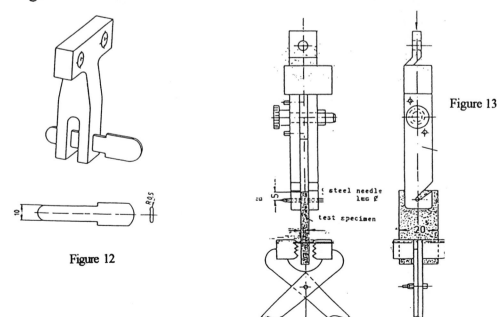

Figure 12

steel needle 1⌀ ⌀

test specimen

Figure 13

Testing of adhesion of finish (IUF 470) needs a holder and a linking hook to assemble, as shown in figures 14 and 15.

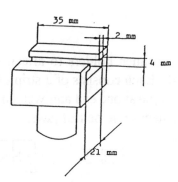

35 mm
2 mm
4 mm
21 mm

Figure 14
Holder

Minimum
20 cm

Figure 15
Linking hook

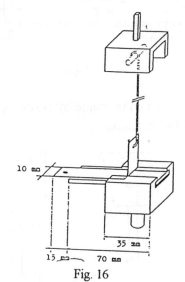

10 mm
35 mm
15 mm
70 mm

Fig. 16
Arrangement of specimen and apparatus
for test

3.   Testing machines and apparatus

IUP 4   Thickness gauge

The instrument used is a dial micrometer type of gauge standing on a firm base. It is dead weight loaded and the load applied is 393 ± 10 g weight (equivalent to 500 g per square centimetre). The presser foot is flat, circular, and of diameter 1.00 cm, and its direction of movement is normal to the face of the anvil. The anvil is the flat, horizontal surface of a cylinder of diameter 1.00 cm, which projects 0.3 cm from the surface of a flat circular platform of diameter 5 cm The axes of the presser foot, the platform and the projecting anvil coincide and are the same as the direction of movement of the foot. The faces of the foot and anvil are parallel for all positions of the foot, the error not exceeding 0.005 mm. The dial gauge is graduated to read 0.01 mm directly. It has a dial of sufficiently large size to give an open scale, and a suitable pointer close to the scale to keep errors due to parallax small. The readings of the gauge are to be accurate to 0.01 mm all along the scale.

In daily practice, a spring thickness gauge may be used.

IUP 6/8   Tensile machine having a uniform speed of separation of the jaws of 100 ± 20 mm per minute.

IUP 7   Kubelka apparatus (can be made with a titration burette and a becher)

IUP 9   Lastometer   SATRA
                                             Rockingham Road Kettering
                                             NORTHANTS NN 16 9JH England

IUP 10   Penetrometer   Bally International
                                             CH - 5012 Schoenenwerd
                                             Switzerland

IUP 11   Permeometer   Bally International
                                             CH - 5012 Schoenenwerd
                                             Switzerland

IUP 13   Tensometer   Bally International
                                             CH - 5012 Schoenenwerd
                                             Switzerland

IUP 20   Flexometer   COMACO
                                             56029 Santa Croce s/Arno (Pi)
                                             Italy

FAMAC
56029 Santa Croce s/Arno (Pi)
Italy

IUP 21	Dome plastometer SATRA	
IUP 26	Sole leather abrasion	Apparatus according ISO 4649
IUC 3	Grinding mill	Mill with a knife velocity of 700-1000 revolutions per minute and a sieve with a 4 mm diameter mesh.
IUF 131 **IUF 132**	Grey scales	Society of Dyers and Colourists P.O.Box 244, Bradford, West Yorkshire BD1 2JB England (many national Standards Institutes)
IUF 401/402 **421/423/434** **435**	Standard blue wool cloths multifibers fabrics	idem
IUF 421	Hydrotest	consists of a stainless steel frame, into which a piston fits precisely, 4.5 kg in weight and 115 x 60 mm in cross-section, and plates of an inert material, e.g. glass of the same area and about 1.5 mm thick. supplier: H. E. Pfister A.G. Seeblickstrasse 20 CH-8731 Uetliburg-Gommiswald Switzerland
IUF 423/ **434**	Wacker apparatus L. Dose K.G.	D- 7581 Grauelsbaum Germany or Launder-Ometer Atlas Electric Devices Co Chicago USA
	or Lintest	Quarzlampen Gesellschaft D - Hanau Germany
IUF 450/454 **458**	Rub tester	VESLIC rub fastness tester is made under VESLIC licence by W. Kueny CH - 4142 Munchenstein Switzerland

BLC leather softness tester
BLC Leather Trade House, Kings Park Road, Moulton Park,
Northhampton NN3 IJD England
designed for commercial production by RWD Bramley

Testing equipment for footwear

SATRA Sole Adhesion tester STD 185
to measure the strength of adhesion on stuck-on and molded soles in the shoe factory or in the
testing laboratory. Attachments for unusual toe shapes, heel adhesion and insole ribs are available.

BIBLIOGRAPHY

- Lange J. Qualitätsbeurteilung von Leder, Lederfehler, Lederlagerung und Lederpflege. Bibliothek des Leders, Band 10. Umschau Verlag. 1982

- Luijten J.A.J. Kwaliteitsrichtlijnen Schoenmaterialen. (Recommendations for footwear materials). TNO Waalwijk, Netherlands

- Reports of meetings of the Commissions of IULTCS

REFERENCES

(1) International Contract No 6 - Annexe C, C1.1 and C4.10 - Annexe D, D1.1 - International Contract No 7 -17, 17.2

(2) Kronick P.and Maleef B. "Nondestructive failure testing of bovine leather by acoustic emission" Journal of the American Leather Chemists Association, JALCA, vol. 87, 1992, No 7, pg. 259.

    Miller R.K., McIntire P. "Nondestructive Testing Handbook, vol. 5. Acoustic emission testing" - American Society for Nondestructive Testing. 1987.

(3) Werner W. Ledertechnik, VEB Fachbuchverlag Leipzig 1979, pg 264.

(4) Fisher W., Schmidt W. Leder und Häutemarkt 1970 pg 13-18

(5) TNO Centre for Leather and Shoe Research, Mr. van Coothstraat 55 NL 5141 ER Waalwijk, The Netherlands

(6) Maiser M. Jalca 1947 pg 390 - Das Leder 1950 pg 46
    Maiser M. Chemistry and Technology of Leather, Vol.4 pg 326.

(7) SATRA Bulletin 3 1978.

(8) Boulanger J. and al. Le Perméabilimètre CTC - Technicuir 7 1974 pg 43.

(9) Kaussen M. Update on the production of automotive leathers
    JALCA Vol.84 1989 pg 353.

(10) Policky F. The challenge of European Automotive Upholstery finishes, JSLTC vol.74 1990 pg 99.

(11) Friese H., Pieper F. Fünf Jahre Erfahrungen mit Fogging-Prüfungen. Das Leder Vol.41 1990 pg 237.

(12) Alexander K., Stosic R. A new non-destructive leather softness test JSLTC vol.77 1993 pg 139

(13) Donmez K. Kallenberger W. Flame resistance of Leather JALCA vol 87 1992 pg 1.

(14) Standard felts may be obtained from Eidgenössische Materialprüfungs-und Forschungsanstalt EMPA, Unterstrasse 11, CH-9001 St. Gallen, Switzerland.

(15) Fisher W., Schmidt W., Das Leder, vol. 27, 1977, pg 175.

(16) Weber W., Das Leder, vol.19, 1969, pg.90-96.

(17) Lange J. Qualitätsbeurteilung von Leder - Bibliothek des Leders, Band 10. Umschauverlag 1982 pg. 178.

(18) To measure the finish adhesion, there is also a simple method in which the force to peel the finish film is exerted by small weight progressively placed on a scale pan. This method is standardized by the British Leather Chemists Society (Test for Adhesion of finish to Leather Draft SLT 11:1992 - JSLTC vol.76 No 6 1992 pg 215).

(19) Fisher W., Schmidt W. Leder & Häutemarkt 1963 G+P pg 72-78.

(20) Fisher W., Schmidt W. "Werkstoffprüfung - Testmethoden und Verfahren" PFI Pirmasens pg.56-57.

(21) Gratacos E. Leder und Häutemarkt 19 pg 504-508.

(22) Kuno, "Human Perspiration" Thomas, Springfield, Ill. USA 1956.

(23) Mitton R. JSLTC, 1950, pg 41-57 - Das Leder 1960, pg 285-293.

(24) Grassmann W., Stadler P. Das Leder 1953, pg 218-228.

(25) Herfeld H., Härtewig K. "Kurzprüfung der Schweissbeständigheit" Leder und Häutemarkt 1960 No 10.

(26) Otto J. Untersuchung und Beurteilung des Leders, 1976, pg 49.

(27) Esche H., Döring E., Chromoxydbestimmung in Leder mit der Röntgen-fluoreszenzanalyse, Das Leder 1993, pg 93.

(28) Stephens L. A simple method for the combined determination of both Zirconium and Aluminium in leather and tanning solutions, JSLTC, vol.71, 1987, pg 10.

(29) Waite T. Tannin analysis - A 130 year problem, JSLTC 1992 pg 187.

(30) Bickley J. Vegetable and Synthetic Tannins, Some notes on procedures for routine analysis, JSLTC 1993, pg 50.

(31) Püntener A. Einige aspekte der analytik von lederfarbstoffen und lederchemikalien, Das Leder 1992, pg 228.

(32) Cot J. and alia, Instrumental techniques for evaluation of residual retanning baths, JSLTC 1991, pg 20.

(33) A procedure for estimation of acrylic syntan strength in tanning liquors, Leather Manufacturer, February 1992, pg 22.

(34) Gnamm H. Die Gerbstoffe und Gerbmittel, Stuttgart 1949.
LIRI, Grahamstown, Wattle tannin and mimosa extract, 1955.

(35) Endres H. and alia, Die Rohstoffe des Planzenreiches, Weinheim 1962

(36) Conseil des Communautés Européennes. Directive du Conseil concernant le PCP -Bulletin des Communautés NG. L 85/34 21 mars 1991

(37) Nickolaus G. Bestimmung kleiner Konzentrationen chlorierter Phenole in Ledern (Determination of Low Levels of PCP in Leather), Das Leder Vol.43 1992 No 1 pg 1.

(38) Muralidharan D. and alia, CLRI Madras and Nickolaus G. PFI Pirmasens, An innovative chromatographic technique for PCP analysis XXII IULTCS Congress Proceedings, Porto Alegre Brazil 1993 Vol 2, pg 370.

(39) Prüfverfahren zur "Bestimmung des Gehaltes an Pentachlorophenol in Leder DIN 53 313 E 10/93 - Beuth Verlag, Berlin

(40) Verdu E. and alia, Determination of PCP in footwear leathers' AQEIC Boletin 1993,pg 14.

(41) Bailey D., Miller R. Residual preservatives in crust leather, JALCA 1991, pg 185.

(42) Tomaselli M., Cozzolino A., Liccardi C. Cuoio vol. 66, No 3 pg 129 Pesticides used in the leather industry - Quantitative Detection.

(43) Mozersky S., Bailey D. Hide powder azure and azocoll as substrates for assay of proteolytic activity of bate, JALCA 1992, pg 287.

(44) Marjoniemi M., Mäntysalo E. Studies on multicomponent spectroscopic analysis of dye solutions, JALCA 1992, pg 249.

(45) White P., Macpherson W. Spectrometric characterisation of Dyes by peak purity parameter, JSLTC abstracts 1993, pg 21.

(46) Eitel K. Das Färben von Leder - Bibliothek des Leders, Umschau Verlag. pg 186.

(47) ibidem pg 185.

(48) Lach D. Various methods to control the quality of dyestuffs and pigments, JALCA 1989 pg 204.

(49) Püntener A. and alia, How to test for Benzidine dyes in dye mixtures, JSLTC vol 77, 1993, pg 1.

(50) Tomaselli M. and alia - Determination of Benzidine and other aromatic amines in dyestuffs and dyed leathers - Proceedings of the XXII IULTCS Congress, Po Alegre Brazil, 1943, Vol 2 pg 539.

(51) TEGEWA, Prüfmethoden für Technische Lieferbedingungen und Kendaten für Zurichtprodukten, Das Leder vol 78, April 1994, pg 84.

(52) SLTC Chemical Analysis Committee, JSLTC 1988 pg 59.
      Analysis of pickled pelt.

(53) SATRA Communication.

(54) Peet M. SATRA, "Developments in Shoe Components", World Footwear, 1993, pg. 8.

(55) Fisher B. Revisions to ISO 9000 Quality Standards, World Footwear, May/June 1994.

(56) ISO, Assessment and verification of conformity to standards and technical specifications, 1992.

(57) ITC Geneve, ISO 9000 quality management systems, guidelines for enterprises in developing countries (available in English, French and Spanish).

(58) Lange J. Qualitätssicherung von Möbelledern und Ledermöbeln, Leder- und Häutemarkt, February 1980.

(59) Schmél F. Industrial Development Officer, UNIDO.

UNIDO GENERAL STUDIES SERIES

The following publications are available in this series:

Title	Symbol	Price (US$)
Planning and Programming the Introduction of CAD/CAM Systems A reference guide for developing countries	ID/SER.O/1	25.00
Value Analysis in the Furniture Industry	ID/SER.O/2	7.00
Production Management for Small- and Medium-Scale Furniture Manufacturers A manual for developing countries	ID/SER.O/3	10.00
Documentation and Information Systems for Furniture and Joinery Plants A manual for developing countries	ID/SER.O/4	20.00
Low-cost Prefabricated Wooden Houses A manual for developing countries	ID/SER.O/5	6.00
Timber Construction for Developing Countries Introduction to wood and timber engineering	ID/SER.O/6	20.00
Timber Construction for Developing Countries Structural timber and related products	ID/SER.O/7	25.00
Timber Construction for Developing Countries Durability and fire resistance	ID/SER.O/8	20.00
Timber Construction for Developing Countries Strength characteristics and design	ID/SER.O/9	25.00
Timber Construction for Developing Countries Applications and examples	ID/SER.O/10	20.00
Technical Criteria for the Selection of Woodworking Machines	ID/SER.O/11	25.00
Issues in the Commercialization of Biotechnology	ID/SER.O/13	45.00
Software Industry Current trends and implications for developing countries	ID/SER.O/14	25.00
Maintenance Management Manual With special reference to developing countries	ID/SER.O/15	35.00
Manual for Small Industrial Businesses Project design and appraisal	ID/SER.O/16	25.00
Policies for Competition and Competitiveness Case-study of industry in Turkey	ID/SER.O/17	35.00
From Waste to Profits Experiences, Guidelines, Film	ID/SER.O/19	75.00
Acceptable Quality Standards in the Leather and Footwear Industry	ID/SER.O/20	30.00

Forthcoming titles include:

Design and Manufacture of Bamboo and Rattan Furniture	ID/SER.O/12	
Manual on Technology Transfer Negotiations	ID/SER.O/18	
Information Sources on the Leather, Footwear and Leather Products Industry	ID/SER.O/21	
Guidelines for the Development, Negotiation and Contracting of Build-Operate-Transfer (BOT) Projects	ID/SER.O/22	

Please add US$ 2.50 per copy to cover postage and packing. Allow 4-6 weeks for delivery.

ORDER FORM

Please complete this form and return it to:

Distribution Unit (F-355)
Vienna International Centre
P.O. Box 300, A-1400 Vienna, Austria

Send me _____ copy/copies of _____

_____ (ID/SER.O/_____) at US$ _____ /copy plus postage.

PAYMENT

☐ I enclose a cheque, money order or UNESCO coupon (obtainable from UNESCO offices worldwide) made payable to "UNIDO".

☐ I have made payment through the following UNIDO bank account: CA-BV, No. 29-05115 (ref. RB-7310000), Schottengasse 6, A-1010 Vienna, Austria.

Name _____

Address _____

Telephone _____ Telex _____ Cable _____ Fax_____

Note: Publications in this series may also be obtained from:

Sales Section
United Nations
Room DC2-0853
New York, N.Y. 10017, U.S.A.
Tel.: (212) 963-8302

Sales Unit
United Nations
Palais des Nations
CH-1211 Geneva 10, Switzerland
Tel.: (22) 34-60-11, ext. Bookshop

-- ✂

ORDER FORM

Please complete this form and return it to:

Distribution Unit (F-355)
Vienna International Centre
P.O. Box 300, A-1400 Vienna, Austria

Send me _____ copy/copies of _____

_____ (ID/SER.O/_____) at US$ _____ /copy plus postage.

PAYMENT

☐ I enclose a cheque, money order or UNESCO coupon (obtainable from UNESCO offices worldwide) made payable to "UNIDO".

☐ I have made payment through the following UNIDO bank account: CA-BV, No. 29-05115 (ref. RB-7310000), Schottengasse 6, A-1010 Vienna, Austria.

Name _____

Address _____

Telephone _____ Telex _____ Cable _____ Fax_____

Note: Publications in this series may also be obtained from:

Sales Section
United Nations
Room DC2-0853
New York, N.Y. 10017, U.S.A.
Tel.: (212) 963-8302

Sales Unit
United Nations
Palais des Nations
CH-1211 Geneva 10, Switzerland
Tel.: (22) 34-60-11, ext. Bookshop